Praise for *Strategy Plain and Simple*

D0795110

'*****! This fast-moving book gives a proven, practical approach that you can apply immediately to start a successful business or build your current business into a lean, mean profit machine.'

Brian Tracy, success guru, speaker and author, *Now Build a Better Business!*

'Clear, straightforward and practical guidance on how to build a business. A must-have for the SME owner or manager.'

James Courtenay, former Global Head of International Corporates, Standard Chartered Bank

'If you are a small business or start up, this is an excellent and admirably succinct guide to help you get your strategy right. Business strategy is all too often discussed in the context of big business. Vaughan Evans, on the other hand, makes it relevant to SMEs, demonstrating not only why but how to develop the right strategy to succeed.'

Anthony Karibian, founder and CEO, bOnline; founder, XLN and Euroffice

'A concise and compelling insight into strategy development, one of the key success factors in every business, large or small.'

Mike Garland, former Partner and Head of Portfolio Group, Permira Advisers LLP

'Vaughan Evans is adept at demystifying strategy and business planning. Here he distils business strategy for the SME into three steps, in a short, punchy, practical book. Ideal for the time-poor entrepreneur.'

Jeff van der Eems, former Chief Executive Officer, United Biscuits

'Strategy in a nutshell, tailor-made for the small businessperson.'

James Pitt, Partner, Lexington Partners

'If you want to take your start-up or small business to the next level, you need a strategy. This can often seem complex – but not so with this compact book. Vaughan Evans does what he says on the tin – he keeps it plain and simple.'

Stephen Lawrence, Chairman, Protocol Education; former Managing Director, Arthur D. Little

'Bite-sized strategy for the small businessperson – crisp, concise and readily digested on one plane journey!'

David Williamson, Managing Partner, Nova Capital Management

'Every business needs a strategy, but many entrepreneurs can't find the time to develop one – let alone digest a formidable tome on how to do it. Vaughan Evans provides the answer: *Strategy Plain and Simple* keeps it, well, plain and simple – and short. Just the job!'

Merric Mercer, CEO, Hive Ltd

'A straightforward and practical framework for developing your business strategy. This book breaks down what can be a daunting task into a step by step guide that really works.'

Andrew Ferguson, Managing Director, UK Private Equity, Baird Capital

'Small business owners or managers lack one precious commodity: time. Managing the now often means tomorrow, with strategy put on the back-burner – they know it should be done, but when and how? They have no director of strategy because the business is too small – and when can they find the time to learn about strategy? *Strategy Plain and Simple* breaks that deadlock. Vaughan Evans replaces the heavy theory associated with strategy books with a short, sharp, three-stage approach, along with vivid examples, tips and charts—and all conveyed in a lively, engaging writing style. This book is a must-read for the small businessperson. Take it off the shelf, read, apply and profit.'

Grahame Hughes, founder and Director, Haven Power

'A most concise, practical and readable guide for those starting or growing their own business and looking to apply sound logical principles to the task of strategic planning.'

Ben Johnson, Partner, Vitruvian Partners

'I used a book by Vaughan Evans chapter-by-chapter to write a detailed three-year business plan for my company. In this book he fleshes out the strategy chapter and provides a range of practical tools to help you understand the strengths of your business, the relative threat posed by your competitors and how to prioritise specific segments of your business. He illustrates all these with an array of lively and pertinent case studies – and all in 150 pages or so! This book is a really useful tool.'

Richard Jewell, Business Development Director, The Key

'This is a highly practical and most succinct guide to drawing up a strategy for any business. It is an enjoyable read, packed with colourful examples that bring the theory to life in a highly user-friendly manner.'

Paul Gough, Managing Partner, STAR Capital Partnership

'Vaughan Evans advocates that strategy should be kept simple – otherwise how can an entrepreneur or manager explain it convincingly to potential investors? Here he offers a straightforward, no nonsense approach that works. It is a gem of a book.'

Christine Harvey, former Director of Business Analysis and Planning, GlaxoSmithKline R&D

'This is an excellent little book for the time-short entrepreneur or manager tasked with defining a strategy for their business, one geared towards meeting the exacting demands of investors like ourselves. Invaluable.'

Bill Priestley, Chief Investment Partner, Epiris

'I have not met many entrepreneurs who actually enjoy taking out the time needed to work out a proper strategy for their business. After all, we could use that time to make some sales calls, think up some new ideas... and the list goes on. However, Vaughan Evans shows here that a sound strategy is not only essential for success but can also be a whole lot of fun – especially when it helps you raise the capital you need to start or grow your business. This highly readable pocket book will prove useful for both new and experienced entrepreneurs.'

Loxley McKenzie, Managing Director, Colordarcy Investment Limited

'Vaughan Evans's ultra-concise, clear and accessible guide to the whats, whys and hows of strategy development will be a huge boon to time-deprived SME executives.'

Richard Kemp, Managing Partner, Sephton Capital

'If you want investment, you must have a robust strategy – one which will convince your backer that you can and will grow the business. This book shows you, simply and succinctly, how to do it.'

Jonathan Derry-Evans, Partner, Manfield Partners

Strategy
Plain and
Simple

Strategy Plain and Simple

3 steps to building a successful strategy for your startup or growing business

Vaughan Evans

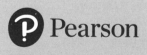 Pearson

Harlow, England • London • New York • Boston • San Francisco • Toronto • Sydney
Dubai • Singapore • Hong Kong • Tokyo • Seoul • Taipei • New Delhi
Cape Town • São Paulo • Mexico City • Madrid • Amsterdam • Munich • Paris • Milan

Pearson Education Limited
KAO Two
KAO Park
Harlow CM17 9NA
United Kingdom
Tel: +44 (0)1279 623623
Web: www.pearson.com/uk

First edition published 2018 (print and electronic)

ISBN: 978-1-292-21813-7 (print)
      978-1-292-21814-4 (PDF)
      978-1-292-21815-1 (ePub)

British Library Cataloguing-in-Publication Data
A catalogue record for the print edition is available from the British Library

Library of Congress Cataloging-in-Publication Data
A catalog record for the print edition is available from the Library of Congress

10 9 8 7 6 5 4 3 2 1
21 20 19 18 17

Cover design by Two Associates
Print edition typeset in 9/13pt Helvetica Neue LT W1G by iEnergizer Aptara®, Ltd.
Print edition printed by Ashford Colour Press Ltd, Gosport
NOTE THAT ANY PAGE CROSS REFERENCES REFER TO THE PRINT EDITION

Contents

About the author / xiii

Acknowledgements / xiv

Preface / xv

Introduction / xvii

On plain and simple strategy / xvii

Getting ready – knowing your business / xx

Identifying key segments / xx

Apple's super segments / xxii

Segmentation in a startup / xxiii

Getting ready – taking aim / xxv

Setting long-term goals / xxvi

Life at Mars / xxviii

Setting SMART objectives / xxx

1   Understanding the market

Forecasting market demand / 3

Sizing the market / 3

Assessing market demand / 8

No wrap for the cinema / 13

Assessing demand for a startup / 15

Assessing industry competition / 18

Checking out your competitors / 19

Gauging competitive intensity / 19

Blockbusted / 21

Identifying customer buying criteria / 22

Deriving factors for success / 25

A sorry affair / 29

Acknowledging competition in a startup / 30

2   **Creating competitive advantage**

Tracking your competitive position / 37

Competitive position in an established
business / 37

Getting past first base / 41

Implications for future market share / 42

Implications for strategy development / 42

Work out and partay?! / 43

Competitive position for a startup / 45

Of dames and detectives / 47

Targeting the strategic gap / 49

Targeting the portfolio gap / 49

Targeting the capability gap / 54

Re-beerth! / 58

Targeting the gap for a startup / 59

Da vino a gelato / 61

Bridging the gap: business strategy / 63

Opting for a generic strategy / 64

Nets working / 67

Strategic repositioning and shaping profit
growth options / 68

Grouping into strategic alternatives / 74

ENT-erprise! / 75

Making the strategic investment decision / 78
One happy Christmas / 81
Bridging the gap for a startup / 81

Bridging the gap: corporate strategy / 84
Optimising the corporate portfolio / 85
Fire sale at Ford / 90
Creating value through mergers, acquisitions
and alliances / 91
'There is a tide . . .' / 93
Building strategically valuable resources / 95

3   Managing risk

Assessing the balance of risk and
opportunity / 99
Extraordinary risk / 100
The balance of risk / 101
Britney does it again / 104

Containing risk / 107

Conclusion / 109
Appendices

The Strategy Pyramid / 110
Cracking the jargon / 113
Ten books to read next / 115
Index / 116

About the author

Vaughan Evans is an independent consultant specialising in strategy and business planning for SMEs and in strategic due diligence for private equity clients.

An economics graduate from the University of Cambridge and a Sloan fellow with distinction from London Business School, Vaughan worked for many years at international management and technology consultants Arthur D. Little and at investment bankers Bankers Trust Co.

He is the author of a number of successful books on strategy and business planning, including the best-selling *Financial Times Essential Guide to Writing a Business Plan: How to Win Backing to Start Up or Grow Your Business* (Pearson, 2nd edition 2016).

Vaughan is also a charismatic and enthralling speaker and seminar leader. His keynote speech on *KISSTRATEGY*, how to keep strategy simple, yet backable, is as instructive as it is entertaining. He is the author of the pithy, witty, yet enlightening *Stand, Speak, Deliver!: How to Survive – and Thrive – in Public Speaking and Presenting* (Little Brown, 2015).

Find out more at www.vaughanevansandpartners.com

Acknowledgements

We are grateful to the following for permission to reproduce copyright material:

Figure 2.11 adapted from BCG Portfolio Matrix, © The Boston Consulting Group (BCG).

Preface

Let me start with a plea: do not buy this book if you are looking for in-depth, innovative, path-breaking strategic analysis. I don't want you telling me off on Amazon for trotting out tired old business concepts, revealing nothing new!

This is strategy plain and simple. No more, no less.

It is aimed at small to medium-sized businesspersons or managers of sizeable businesses within a larger company, wishing to take their business from where it is today to where they want it to be tomorrow.

It is not aimed at managers of multinational or global corporations. It is not aimed at business school graduates thirsty for new strategic thinking as they pursue their careers in consulting or investment banking.

It is aimed at the everyman businessman and the everywoman businesswoman.

Strategy can be complex, and it is in the evident self-interest of academics and consultants to make it so. But for most of the time and for most businesses, the concepts need not be complex. The basics are quite straightforward.

At the back of this book I shall point you in the direction of further reading, if you find yourself in need of it.

In the meantime, this book portrays strategy at its simplest and plainest.

It cuts strategy to the quick – the very essence of what you need to know to draw up a strategy for your business.

It is as light on the theory as is possible, while still conveying the message.

It strives to be jargon-free.

It illustrates each section with lively examples from the world of business – be they in British gyms, Spanish beer, Italian ice cream, US healthcare, Australian networking, Canadian dating or other markets.

Where possible, it uses charts rather than words – streamlining the message.

It is written for those who, typically, have little time to read a business book – and, when they do, they want the message conveyed as plainly and as quickly as possible. It is, therefore, short – more or less readable on one train or plane journey.

Enjoy!

Introduction

In the introduction you will find:

- On plain and simple strategy
- Getting ready – knowing your business
- Getting ready – taking aim

On plain and simple strategy

Simplicity is the ultimate sophistication.

Leonardo da Vinci

First things first. Why should you, an entrepreneur or manager, draw up a strategy? What is it? Why does your firm need it?

The answer is simple: strategy is what you need to get your business from where you are today to where you want it to be in a few years' time.

But, you might say, why do I need a strategy to do that? The business can just carry on what it is doing now, maybe introduce a new product here, enter a new market there and, in three years' time, we should have larger profits than we have today.

Fine. You have a strategy. It is called 'seat-of-the-pants'. Your business is at the mercy of the market. If demand takes a dip, or if customers switch to a substitute offering, your revenues will tumble. Likewise, if a competitor comes up with a superior or cheaper product or radically improves standards of service.

And what if you launch a new product that is super but fails to excite your customers?

The market may remain favourable. You may make the right investment calls. You may achieve your hoped-for profits in year 3. But that is called luck.

Strategy is about reducing dependence on luck.

It is about guiding your company to the next level – while recognising what is happening in the market, making the most of your company's capabilities and managing risk to acceptable levels.

More specifically, and technically, strategy is about how you deploy your firm's scarce resources to develop an enduring competitive advantage – and thereby achieve your goals and objectives.

Every company, from the corner tyre repair shop to Apple Inc., needs a strategy. Without one, you will be floating on a wing and a prayer.

With a strategy, you have a better chance of getting to where you want to go.

And the good news is that it does not have to be that complex to draw one up.

It was the US Navy in the 1960s that reportedly coined the KISS principle. 'Keep it simple, stupid' was adopted as the principle on which the design of naval warplanes should be based – and for obvious reasons: the simpler the design, the less complex the engineering, the more likely engineers stationed at sea on aircraft carriers, far from sophisticated onshore repair and mainte- nance facilities, would be able to fix problems themselves.

In this book I have applied the KISS principle to strategy development. I looked at the Strategy Pyramid approach I developed in earlier books (see Appendix A) and stripped it back to its bare essentials.

In particular, I strived to reduce the number of parts or components of strategy development to *three* – for this is the number of items that psychologists tell us can be related to *and remembered* readily by the average person.

I found that it was, indeed, possible. And simple. This is it:

Developing strategy

=

Understanding the market

+

Creating competitive advantage

+

Managing risk

Even plainer, leaving out the verbs:

Strategy = Market + Advantage + Risk

This can be portrayed in a diagram of building blocks, as in the following figure.

Strategy Plain and Simple

This is strategy kept simple. Building on the US military maxim of KISS, I have elsewhere called it KISSTRATEGY.

The parts are sequential. Understanding the market must come first. It underpins strategy development. It should be the horse to the strategy cart.

Managing risk is the trailer behind the cart. It represents the fine-tuning of strategy.

Creating competitive advantage, a sustainable advantage, is the cargo on the cart, the essence of strategy.

But, before we embark on the first stage, understanding the market, we need to do some preparation. We need to get ready ...

Getting ready – knowing your business

Before getting started on your strategy development, pause for a while.

In which cupboards of your business do the profits reside?

You need to know your business. You need to clarify the major business segments in which you compete and those that contribute most, both to the top line and to the bottom line. Now and in the future.

If your business is a startup, you need to do the same. But we will start with identifying key segments in an established business.

Identifying key segments

Does your firm serve some segments where you generate good sales but frustratingly little profit? And what of those merrier segments where sales are modest but margins meaty?

Step one in strategy development is to know your business, where the profit resides.

There are three components to this:

- Which business segments does your firm compete in – which products* do you sell to which sets of customers?
- Which of these segments delivers the most profit?
- How may this change over time?

*Or services, but we will call them 'products' in this section

Only once you have completed this segmentation should you embark on developing your strategy. There is no point devoting hours of research, whether in analysing competitor data or gathering customer feedback, on a segment that contributes to just 1 per cent of your operating profit – and that offers little prospect of growing that contribution over the next five years.

How you could strengthen your capabilities in that segment may be fascinating but is not material to your business strategy and of little interest to your board or backer.

You need to devote your time and effort to strengthening your firm's presence in those segments that contribute, or will contribute, to 80 per cent or more of your business.

First, then, what is your business mix? What products or services does your business sell and to which customer groups? Which count for most in your business?

Businesses seldom offer just the one product to one customer group. Most businesses offer a number of distinct products to a number of distinct customer groups, reachable through differing marketing approaches.

Each distinct product offered to a distinct customer group is a segment. Which segments contribute most to your firm's sales? How has the contribution of key segments to sales changed over the last few years? And how may it change over the next few years?

You may find it helpful to present that data in a pie chart, as in the following figure.

Business mix

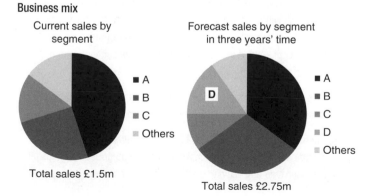

Current sales by segment

- A
- B
- C
- Others

Total sales £1.5m

Forecast sales by segment in three years' time

D

- A
- B
- C
- D
- Others

Total sales £2.75m

And what about profit? Which segments contribute most to gross profit? And, if you have the data, or you can make reasonable estimates of the breakdown of overheads, which contribute most to operating profit?

How has the contribution of key segments to operating profit changed over the last few years? And how may it change over the next few years?

Pop the profit data by segment into another couple of pie charts and compare them with those for revenue. What does that tell you?

This segmentation analysis will give you the base understanding of your business upon which to develop your strategy.

SIMPLE TIP

Be careful of paralysis through analysis. Do not end up with dozens of segments. Concentrate on the half-dozen or so that truly drive your firm's operating profit.

APPLE'S SUPER SEGMENTS

What will be the next Apple blockbuster product? Will there be one? The stock market seems to think so.

In the 1990s, Apple was a manufacturer of personal computers, one with a devoted following, but not large enough to prevent it from struggling financially. Sales started to decline in 1995 and were not to reach those levels again until 2005, during which time it recorded either low or negative profitability.

Yet Apple went on to become the most valuable company in history, topping $800 billion in May 2017. How did that happen?

A segmentation of Apple's business in the late 1990s would have shown a broad range of Macintosh personal computers, categorised perhaps by product, user type and region. The PCs were facing tough competition from IBM and its many clones, now with an improved graphical user interface and running a superior operating system, Microsoft. Market share was eroding.

One new segment showed promise – a personal digital assistant, the Newton. Another was even more embryonic – a portable digital audio player, to be called the iPod, linking it to the promising flashy redesign of the Macintosh, the iMac.

The iPod turned the tide and lead to iTunes, a revolution in music industry online distribution. Then came the real sensation, the iPhone, a device that blended stylishly the capabilities of mobile phone, digital audio/video player and digital camera. Later Apple launched the iPad, a tablet computer that seemed destined to cannibalise other lines but succeeded in creating its very own category.

Personal computers now comprise just 11 per cent of Apple's sales (Q2, 2017). Two-thirds of sales come from the iPhone and related products and services, which have largely cannibalised the iPod (down to 4 per cent).

Drawing up Apple's strategy for the next few years will not be easy. How to withstand competition from Samsung, HTC and others in the smartphone market will be tough enough, but what about the next big thing?

Apple's strategists will need to take extra care with segmentation. Which product will be the next iPod? Apple Watch? Apple TV? An iPhantastic challenge.

Segmentation in a startup

If you are starting a new venture, you may still need to segment – unless you are launching just the one product (or service) to one group of customers.

But are you sure you will have only the one product? Or one customer group?

Try categorising your products. And your customers. Is further segmentation meaningful? If so, use it. If not, do not waste time just for the sake of seeming serious. Stick to the one product for the one customer group, i.e. one business segment.

But there is one big difference in a startup. No matter how you segment, no matter how many customer groups you identify, they are all, at present, gleams in the eye.

You have no customers. Yet.

Your product must be couched in terms of its benefits to the customer. That is the business proposition.

Not the way in which your product can do this, do that, at this price. But the way in which your product or service can *benefit* the target customer.

Who is the target customer? In which way will he or she benefit from your offering?

And that is just in the one segment. Are there others?

Segmentation may lie at the very heart of your business proposition. It may have been how you unearthed a niche where only your offering can yield benefit to the customer.

For further stimulating thoughts on this, see the section on 'Will the fish bite?' in John Mullins' indispensable guide to business startups, *The New Business Road Test: What Entrepreneurs and Executives Should Do Before Writing a Business Plan*.

Here is a slightly different way of looking at it. Does your offering address some 'unmet need' in the marketplace? Does it fill a gap in a target customer's needs? This is one of the secrets to a new venture's success highlighted by William Bridges in his book, *Creating You & Co*. He suggests that an 'unmet need' could be uncovered by spotting signs such as a missing piece in a pattern, an unrecognised opportunity, an underused resource, a signal event, an unacknowledged change, a supposedly impossible situation, a non-existent but needed service, a new or emerging problem, a bottleneck, an interface or other similar signs.

However you define the customer benefit, whether in terms of an unmet need or in a way more meaningful to your offering, you need to undertake some basic research (see page 47) to dig up whatever evidence you can glean of likely customer benefit.

This may help you clarify segmentation in your startup.

Getting ready – taking aim

Where do you want your business to be in three to five years' time? What sort of a firm do you want it to be? On which parameters will you measure performance success? What are the aims of your firm?

There are numerous treatises written on the relative merits of a company articulating its vision, mission, aims, purposes, goals, objectives, values, principles, ideals, beliefs, principles and so on. The sound of hair splitting can be deafening.

It is simpler and adequate to stick to two of these: goals and objectives.

A goal is something your business aims to be, as described in words. An objective is a target that helps to measure whether that goal is achieved, and is typically set out in numbers.

One of your goals may be for your business to be the most customer-centric provider of your services in your region. Objectives to back up that goal could be the achievement of a 'highly satisfied' rating of 30 per cent from your annual customer survey by 2015 and 35 per cent by 2017, along with 80 per cent 'satisfied' or better by that year.

Goals are directional, objectives are specific. The former should look beyond the short term and set out where you see the firm in the long term. The latter should be SMART, namely specific, measurable, attainable, relevant and time-limited – more about this later in this section.

Other aims can readily slot into the simple goals and objectives framework:

- **Mission** – in theory, what sets your business apart from the rest of the competition; in practice, you can treat this as a goal.
- **Vision** – in theory, where your business aims to go or become; again, you can treat this as another goal.

- **Aims** (or purposes) – they can be taken as roughly synonymous with goals.

- **Values** (or beliefs, ideals or principles) – in theory, a set of beliefs and principles that guide how your business should respond when there are moral, ethical, safety, health, environmental or other value-related demands on the business that may conflict with the goal of shareholder value maximisation; in practice, this can be identified as a separate goal.

The setting of long-term goals and SMART objectives are essential tools in strategy development.

SIMPLE TIP

Should your over-riding goal be maximising shareholder value in your company? To what extent should you also be striving to serve the interests of other stakeholders, such as employees, customers, the community and the environment?

It is your call. There is an inescapable trade-off. But remember that without shareholder value you have no business. And that would benefit no one – not you, your employees, your customers, not even the taxman – other than your competitors.

Setting long-term goals

Goal setting is at the cornerstone of business strategy. Goals should underpin each of your company's main strategic initiatives over the next five years or so.

Here are the main considerations when setting goals:

- Goals differ from objectives.

- Goals should be long-term – short-term goals have little place in strategy development.

- The best goals are also motivational.

- Financial goals may need to resolve the shareholder–stakeholder trade-off.

- Value-related goals are no less valid.

A goal is something your business aims to be, as described in words. An objective is a target that helps to measure whether that goal is achieved and, typically, is set out in numbers. Your goal may be to become a low-cost provider in a key segment. An accompanying objective might be to reduce unit operating costs in that segment within three years by 15 per cent.

Second, think of short-term goals as what lies within and behind this year's budget. These may be important in the short term, whether for keeping the financial markets or your owners happy or for you landing that performance-related bonus.

But what lies within that budget may have little impact on strategy development. Strategy takes into account market demand trends and industry competition forces that go well beyond the short term. It is no good gearing up your business to compete ferociously in the short term only to be exposed to a drop-off in demand or lowered competitiveness in the medium to long term – see the following figure.

Setting long-term goals

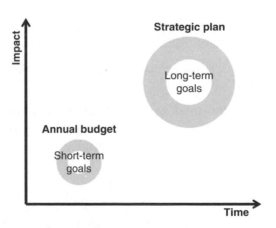

Third, goal setting should also prove motivational. Market- or customer-oriented goals are often the most motivational for the sales force and are easy enough to monitor. Market share data is readily collected by companies beyond a certain size. A goal could be market leadership in a particular segment within three years.

Customer satisfaction or retention goals (or objectives – see the next tool) can also have the same effect.

Operational goals are also incentivising for the operations team – and even simpler to monitor than market-related goals. A goal of cost leadership in a segment within five years, for example, could dynamise a performance improvement team. Progress within the company on unit cost reduction could be tracked over time and compared at annual intervals with the competition.

SIMPLE TIP

Do not have too many goals. They say people cannot remember more than three of any list, but you may choose to stretch that to four or five.

Go for a dozen and you will be lucky to attain half of them. Go for a handful and you may bag the lot.

LIFE AT MARS

What Hoover is to the vacuum cleaner market so, arguably, is Mars to the chocolate bar.

Yet there is much more to Mars Inc. than its eponymous chocolate bar. It was not even its launch product – that was the Milky Way bar. Many people do not even know that Milky Way belongs to Mars Inc., let alone M&Ms.

Most are also unaware that chocolate confectionery is but one slice of a huge, low-key, private company, turning over $33 billion and employing 75,000, with six strategic business units – chocolate, petcare, chewing gum, food, drink and life sciences – despite these units selling such well-known international brands as Pedigree Chum, Wrigley's gum and Uncle Ben's.

That is because Mars Inc. remains a privately owned – and private – company. There are shades of its founders, father Frank and son Forrest Mars, in the company's five core principles of doing business:

- Quality – the consumer is our boss, quality is our work and value for money is our goal.

- Responsibility – as individuals, we demand total responsibility from ourselves; as Associates, we support the responsibility of others.

- Mutuality – a mutual benefit is a shared benefit; a shared benefit will endure.

- Efficiency – we use resources to the full, waste nothing and do only what we can do best.

- Freedom – we need freedom to shape our future; we need profit to remain free.

Mars Inc. believes that these principles are 'a set of fundamental beliefs that help to shape and define us as a company; they express our vision not only of who we are, but where and what we want to be'.

This is all worthy stuff and perhaps these principles genuinely serve to motivate employees. But try stating some opposites or antonyms against key words, for example:

- Quality – the consumer is our servant [. . .]

- Responsibility – we demand no responsibility from ourselves [. . .]

- Mutuality – our actions should always be at the expense of others [. . .]

- Efficiency – we waste everything [. . .]

- Freedom – we need captivity to shape our future [. . .]

A company with such principles would not survive too long, implying that those of Mars Inc. are self-evident. They represent motherhood and apple pie. Unlike goals and objectives, principles are, typically, of little practical application in strategy development.

But these principles seem to work for Mars Inc. And there may be lessons for others in this proselytising approach to business.

Setting SMART objectives

Objectives are intimately linked to goals. Your firm aims towards a goal, a destination typically articulated in words. Objectives are targets, whether along the route or at the final destination, and are, typically, set out in numbers.

You may aim for the goal of regional market leadership in a key segment by 2020. That is a worthy goal, but a bit too vague for a robust strategy. More precise would be the corresponding objectives of attaining 33 per cent market share by 2019 and 35 per cent by 2020. This objective should help deliver your goal of market leadership in that segment.

Whereas goals are indicative and directional, objectives are precise. You should set objectives that are:

- **S**pecific – a precise number against a particular parameter.

- **M**easurable – that parameter must be quantifiable – for example, a market share percentage in a segment rather than a woolly target such as 'best supplier'.

- **A**ttainable – there is no point in aiming for the improbable – disappointment will be the inevitable outcome.

- **R**elevant – the objective should relate to the goal; if the goal is market leadership, an objective of winning 'best marketing campaign of the year' in the trade journal would be inappropriate.

- **T**ime-limited – you should specify by when the objective should be achieved; an objective with no time limitation would serve no motivational purpose and result in the slippage of difficult decisions.

Objectives should be *SMART* – see the following figure. The best objectives are indeed smart. As in the regional market leadership example above, the objectives are: *specific* (a market share target in that segment), *measurable* (market research to which you subscribe will reveal whether the 35 per cent is met), *attainable* (you are at 29 per cent now and your new product range has been well received), *relevant* (market share is the ultimate measure of market leadership) and *time-limited* (2020).

Setting SMART objectives

Specific ✓
Measurable ✓
Attainable ✓
Relevant ✓
Time-limited ✓

As with goal setting, keep it simple. One or two objectives against each of four to five goals should be fine.

OK, you have segmented the business and you have set your long-term goals and SMART objectives.

You are ready to build a plain and simple strategy.

SIMPLE TIP

Here is another take on the same theme. Richard Rumelt, in his best-selling book of 2011, *Good Strategy, Bad Strategy*, states that strategy implementation is greatly assisted by the identification of 'proximate objectives'. Each of these is a target that is close enough that the firm 'can reasonably be expected to hit, or even overwhelm it'. He is emphasising the attainable ('A') component of a SMART objective.

He cites the example of President Kennedy pledging to place a man on the Moon. The objective sounded fanciful, but it was politically inspirational, conveying both national pride and ambition. And Kennedy had an ace up his sleeve – he knew that the technology already existed for such a mission to succeed.

1

Understanding the market

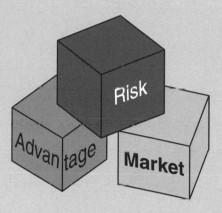

Time spent on reconnaissance is seldom wasted.

Military maxim

- Forecasting market demand
- Assessing industry competition

The market lies at the bedrock of strategy. A strategy that is built upon a solid understanding of the market is like a house built on a concrete foundation.

A strategy that is premised on how wonderful your business offering is, and hang the market, is like a house built on sand. It will be washed away.

To paraphrase the famous military maxim, time spent on understanding the market is seldom wasted.

There are two sides of the market that need to be tackled: demand and supply.

The supply side deals with production and the forces driving competition between the producers, thus determining outcomes such as market share, pricing and profitability.

But let us start with the demand side – how to size market demand and how to forecast where it is headed.

Forecasting market demand

It's better to have the wind at your back than in your face.

Unattributed

How big is the market your firm is addressing? What factors have been influencing demand growth? How are these factors changing? By how much will demand grow in the future? What are the risks?

These are the questions you need answers to. And you need to answer them for each of your main business segments – those you have already identified.

Sizing the market

Size is important.

Without market size you may find it hard to gauge market demand growth. And you certainly will not know market share. Without market share, it is hard to judge competitive position. Then you may find it hard to draw up a winning strategy.

The larger your company, the easier it is to find data on market size. Industry associations proliferate and many either compute market share themselves or contract out the job to specialist market research firms. The latter compete fiercely with one another to cover each and every market where they perceive there to be a sufficient number of customers to turn a profit.

SMEs do not enjoy such lavish attention from market research firms. Some do, and I am often pleasantly surprised when a client turning over £10–20 million reveals monthly market data provided to the firm and its half dozen competitors by some enterprising market research house, often a one-man band.

But most SMEs do not have access to market data. And they are not alone. A medium-sized firm turning over £100 million may well have the bulk of its business covered by market research reports, but not necessarily that star business segment turning over £8 million, with only two main competitors and growing at 25 per cent/year. That segment may as yet be too small with too few potential customers to entice a market researcher.

Where no data on market size can be found off the shelf, you should try to size the market yourself.

First you must decide what you are looking for: your addressed market or your addressable market. The difference can be huge:

● Addressed market – those to whom you currently offer your goods or services and who may or may not purchase them.

● Addressable (or available) market – all those whom you *could* serve should you extend your offering.

There are six main ways of sizing a market:

● **Top-down market research** – start with a known, researched market size and chop out inapplicable sections, or make appropriate assumptions on relevant proportions, to drill down to the target market.

● **Bottom-up market research** – take disaggregated data from a market research report and assemble the relevant bits that make up your target market.

● **Bottom-up customer sizing** – estimate how much each major customer spends in this target market and make an allowance for other, minor customers.

● **Bottom-up competitor sizing** (or 'marketcrafting', see below) – estimate the scale of your competitors in the target market.

● **Related market triangulation** – use two, three or more known sizes of related markets to gauge a rough estimate of the target market.

● **Final triangulation** – juggle the estimates from the above sources and subject them to sanity checks (Why the differences? With which method do you feel most confident? On balance, what *feels* right?); consider giving each estimate a reliability rating, work out relative probabilities and compute a weighted average estimate of target market size.

Marketcrafting is a particularly useful method, since it gives you the base data needed not just for market demand analysis (this section) but for industry supply too (next section). It is a technique I developed some years ago for clients who knew their customers and competitors well enough but had no firm grasp on market scale. I have used it mainly in niche markets or in segments of larger markets, but now and again in larger markets too. I recently used it to estimate a market size of around $175 million in a North American engineering segment left curiously unattended by market research groups.

There are seven main steps in marketcrafting:

1   Select your main competitors – those against whom you pitch regularly, those you exhibit alongside at trade shows – and do not forget the foreign competitors, especially those from lower cost countries.

2   Take competitor A: do you think they are selling more or less than you into this market? If less, by how much less, *very roughly*? Are they selling half as much as you? Three quarters? If they sell more than you, by how much more, very roughly? 10 per cent more? A third more? Is there any publicly available information that can guide you on this? Competitor A's sales to this market are unlikely to be available if it is a private company, but employment data can be indicative. What do customers tell you? And suppliers – do they ship more product to A than to you?

3   Taking your current sales level as an index number of 100, assign the appropriate index number to competitor A; if you think they sell less than you in this market, but not that much less, say 10 per cent less, give them an index number of 90.

4   Repeat steps 2 and 3 for each of the competitors named in step 1.

5   Make an allowance for any other competitors you have not named, those who are small or those who appear only now and again; this should also be

an index number; if you think all these others together sell about half what you sell to the market, give this 'Others' category an index number of 50.

6 Add up all the index numbers, divide the total by 100 and multiply by your level of sales – that is your preliminary estimate of market size.

7 Ask your sales director to do the same exercise; get her to talk to the guy in the sales team who used to work at competitor A and the woman in R&D whose boyfriend's cousin works at competitor B; get their inputs, those of your operations director, and head of R&D; where their views differ from yours, discuss and refine the numbers; now you have built a reasoned estimate of market size.

Marketcrafting is hardly an accurate process, nor can it be guaranteed that the final number will not be some way out. But it is better than nothing, very much better, because you can now use the results to get values of three parameters key to strategy development:

● **Market growth** – repeat the marketcrafting exercise above to estimate the market size of three years ago; for example, did competitor A sell more or less than you to this market three years ago, before that new plant came into operation, and by how much, and so on; you now have two data points – market size of today and that of three years ago; punch them into your calculator and out will come an average compound growth rate over the three years, an estimate of recent market growth.

● **Market share** – now you 'know' market size, you also know your market share (your sales level divided by estimated market size); you also have an estimate of the market share of each of your competitors.

● Best of all, **market share change** – you now have your market share of three years ago, as well as that of today, so you have an estimate of your market share gain (or loss), as well as for each of your competitors; these estimates will be most useful in assessing your competitive position later on.

The following figure is an example of the findings that can be deduced from the process, adapted from work on the North American engineering company referred to above.

Marketcrafting: an example

Competitor	Estimated index number for sales (latest year)	Implied market share (%)
The company	= 100	17%
Competitor A	120	21%
Competitor B	85	15%
Competitor group C	125	21%
Competitor group D	65	11%
Competitor E	30	5%
Competitor F	20	3%
Others	40	7%
Total	585	100%

The company's turnover in this segment was about $30 million, so the market size could be estimated at 585/100 × 30, or around $175 million. The company's market share emerged at 17 per cent (100/585), rather lower than the 25 per cent management had quoted prior to the marketcrafting exercise. Likewise, the market share of the Far Eastern competitors, group D, though significant at 21 per cent, did not seem to be as high as the one third quoted rather sensationally in the trade press.

When we repeated the exercise to estimate market size of three years earlier, we found that the market had contracted heavily during the post-credit crunch recession, falling by one third or by roughly 10 per cent/year. Meanwhile, Far Eastern competitors had grown share greatly from 9 per cent to 21 per cent, with corresponding share losses by the domestic players, including that of the company, from 20 per cent to 17 per cent.

These were important findings. The trends were, of course, known beforehand, but their quantification through the marketcrafting method, though very rough, put some of the wilder assertions into perspective and helped focus attention on the strategic challenge ahead.

Assessing market demand

The quote at the beginning of this section, about it being better to have the wind at your back than in your face, is one that is often heard in the business world.

It is a question of odds. You have a better chance of prospering in a market that is growing than one that is shrinking.

Market size is all very well, but what often matters more in strategy development is what the market is doing, where it is going – the dynamics, as opposed to the statics. Is market demand in your main business segments growing, shrinking or flat-lining?

This is the big question. It is not the only one, of course. Equally important, as we will see later on, is the nature of the competition you face and how you are placed to compete. But it is the first big question.

Many years ago, I developed a four-step process for translating market demand trends and drivers into forecasts. I call it the HOOF approach, for two reasons. HDDF, the strict representation of the first letters in each of the four steps, would be a ghastly acronym, unattractive and unmemorable – but, with the appropriate creative licence, the circular O can be borrowed as a lookalike to the semi-circular D!

And, second, because it reminds me fondly of the junior football team I used to coach. No matter how many times I screeched at a couple of players to play the simple ball out of defence, head up, along the ground, to a nearby player, they would blindly HOOF it down the pitch with all their might, as far as their adolescent muscles could propel it!

There are four distinct stages in the HOOF approach to demand forecasting. Get this process right and all falls logically into place. Get it out of step and you may end up with a misleading answer. You need to apply these steps for each of your main business segments.

The four steps are:

1 **Historic growth** – assess how market demand has grown in the past.

2 **Drivers past** – identify what has been driving that past growth.

3 **Drivers future** – assess whether there will be any change in influence of these and other drivers in the future.

4 **Forecast growth** – forecast market demand growth, based on the influence of future drivers.

Let us look at each of these briefly, then at some examples.

1 Historic growth

This is where you need to get some facts and figures. If you have access to market research data, whether on a regular basis or with a one-off purchase, all your needs should be in there. If not, you may have to do some marketcrafting – see above.

Be careful not to fall into the trap of relying on one recent number. Just because demand for a service jumped by, say, 8 per cent last year does not mean that trend growth in that market has been 8 per cent/year. The latest year may have been an aberration. The market may have dipped two years ago, remained static last year and recovered by 8 per cent this year. Average annual growth over the three years might have been only 2 per cent/year.

You should try to get an average annual (compound) growth rate over a number of recent years, preferably the last three or four. As long as there have not been serious annual ups and downs, like there were in the period 2007–11, you can usually get a usable approximation of average annual growth by calculating the overall percentage change in, say, the last four years and then annualising it. If there have been ups and downs, you could try to smooth them out with three-year moving averages before calculating the percentage change.

One word of caution: market demand growth generally is measured, analysed and forecast in real terms. You should take care to understand the differences between these growth rates:

● **In nominal terms,** that is with goods (or services) priced in the money of the day.

● **In real terms,** which is the growth rate in nominal prices deflated by the growth rate in the average prices of goods in that market; this growth rate, as long as the correct deflators are used, should be a measure of volume growth.

You should be consistent and restrict all analysis of comparative market growth rates to those in real terms, here and throughout the strategy development process.

But should you need to proceed to business planning and financial forecasting, you must bring average price forecasts back into the mix. Then your revenue forecasts, as well as the whole income statement, will be able to be compared directly with market growth rate forecasts in nominal prices.

2 Drivers past and present

Once you have uncovered some information on recent market demand growth, find out what has been influencing that growth. Typical factors that influence demand in many markets are:

● Per capita income growth.

● Population growth in general.

● Population growth specific to a market (for example, of pensioners or baby boomers, or general population growth in a particular region).

● Some aspect of government policy or purchasing.

- Changing awareness, perhaps from high levels of promotion by competing providers.

- Business structural shifts (such as towards outsourcing).

- Price change.

- Fashion, even a craze.

- Weather – seasonal variations, but maybe even the longer-term effects of climate change.

Or your sector may be heavily influenced by demand in other sectors, typically customer sectors. Thus the demand for steel is heavily dependent on demand for automobiles, ships, capital goods equipment and construction.

3 Drivers future

Now you need to assess how each of these drivers is likely to develop over the next few years. Are things going to carry on more or less as before for a driver? Or are things going to change significantly?

Will, for instance, immigration continue to drive local population growth? Is the government likely to hike up a local tax? Could this market become less fashionable?

What are the prospects for growth in vertical or complementary sectors?

The most important driver is, of course, the economic cycle. If it seems the economy is poised for a nosedive, that could have a serious impact on demand in your business over the next year or two – assuming your business is relatively sensitive (or 'elastic', in economics-speak) to the economic cycle. Or maybe your business is relatively inelastic, like, for example, in much of the food industry? You may need to think carefully about the timing of the economic cycle and the elasticity of your business.

4 Forecast growth

This is the fun bit. You have assembled all the information on past trends and drivers. Now you can weave it all together, sprinkle it with a large dose of judgement and you have a forecast of market demand – not without risk, not without uncertainty, but a systematically derived forecast nevertheless.

Let us take a simple example of the HOOF approach in action. In one of your business segments, your firm offers a relatively new service to the elderly. Step 1 **(H):** You find that the market has been growing at 5–10 per cent per year over the last few years. Step 2 **(O):** You identify the main drivers as (a) per capita income growth, (b) growth in the elderly population and (c) growing awareness of the service by elderly people. Step 3 **(O):** You believe income growth will continue as before, the elderly population will grow even faster in the future and that awareness can only get more widespread. Step 4 **(F):** You conclude that growth in your market will accelerate and could reach over 10 per cent per year over the next few years.

The HOOF approach is best used diagrammatically. The example above is simple, but becomes even simpler when displayed on a diagram – see the following figure. The impact of each demand driver on demand growth is represented by varying numbers of plus and minus signs or a zero. In this case, you can see that there will be more pluses in the near future than there were in the past, implying that demand growth will accelerate – from the historic 5–10 per cent/year to the future 10 per cent/year plus.

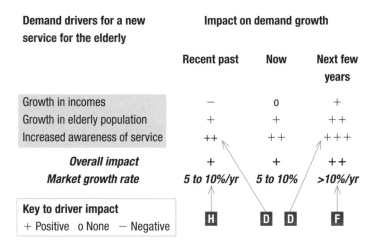

Demand drivers for a new service for the elderly	Impact on demand growth		
	Recent past	**Now**	**Next few years**
Growth in incomes	−	0	+
Growth in elderly population	+	+	++
Increased awareness of service	++	++	+++
Overall impact	+	+	++
Market growth rate	*5 to 10%/yr*	*5 to 10%*	*>10%/yr*

Key to driver impact
+ Positive   o None   − Negative

In real world strategy development, there will be more such charts, one for each key business segment, and each will have more drivers. But the fundamental principles of the HOOF approach will remain. The chart will show the historic growth rate (H), identify the relative impact of drivers past and future (0 & 0) and conclude with a growth forecast for that segment (F).

NO WRAP FOR THE CINEMA

In the mid-1980s, I was tasked to review a business plan for a company intent on developing a string of multiplex cinemas in Britain. The concept had taken off in the USA. Would it work in the UK?

Cinema attendance in the days before television had been an integral part of the British way of life. Numbers peaked at 1.64 billion in post-war 1946 – equivalent to 33 visits to the cinema that year by every man, woman *and child* in the UK! That is one visit every eight or nine days by every single person in the country.

Television changed all that, offering moving picture entertainment from the comfort of the living room. Cinema attendance went on a prolonged downward trend as more and more households acquired the televiewing habit. By the1980s, video ownership and rental had accelerated the decline and the end seemed in sight for the cinema.

By 1984, UK cinema attendances had dropped to 54 million, not much bigger than the 35 million who went to see one film alone, *Gone with the Wind*, in the UK in the 1940s. It had dropped like a stone from 100 million in 1980.

And, yet, there seemed to be some sort of recovery going on. In 1985, attendances had bounced back to 70 million and, in 1986, had consolidated at 73 million. It was 1987 when I looked at this business plan. What was going on? Could the UK cinema industry be reborn?

There were two demand drivers that seemed particularly promising:

● The advent of multiplexes – the first such, The Point in Milton Keynes, with ten screens, had sold 2 million tickets in its first two years and its bustling foyer had become a social meeting point for the youth of the city.

▶

- The upgrading of former flea pits – with consumers in London and other cities seemingly prepared to pay a bit more for a more comfortable and uplifting experience.

But the demand risks remained huge, including:

- Milton Keynes may not be representative of the country as a whole.

- Mutliplexes, if successful, may put small single-screen cinemas out of business, leaving minimal net gain.

- Multiplexes may be a fad.

- DVDs were taking over from video cassettes, raising the prospect of improved quality home movie experience.

- All the socio-economic factors behind the prolonged downward trend in cinema attendances since the 1940s remained.

On balance, it seemed worth the punt. Multiplexes seemed a ray of sunshine. Cinema attendances appeared more likely to maintain their recovery, rather than slip back into decline. But my banking colleagues were more risk-averse and the bank withdrew from the deal.

A bad call. Cinema attendances carried on rising and, by 1990, had recovered to the 100 million level of ten years earlier. And they did not stop there – they carried on growing, with the occasional annual blip, through to a peak of 176 million in 2002. Since then, they have hovered around the 170 million mark, with annual fluctuations tending to reflect the relative success of each year's blockbusters.

Britons now go to the cinema on average three times a year, way, way down on the 1940s, but not too far below the USA at four times and, keenest of all, Iceland at five times.

And what of the future? Positive demand drivers now include luxury cinemas, 3D films and the occasional mega blockbuster. Offset against this are excellent quality large-screen televisions, also with 3D.

Another negative driver is competition not just from television, video, internet and computer games, but also the near video-on-demand offerings of Netflix and Amazon.

Then there is the improved quality of drama series on television, exemplified by *Game of Thrones*. With playback capabilities such as iPlayer and personal video recorders, let alone DVD box sets – and not to mention Illegal downloading – viewers can accumulate so much must-watch past television that they can never find the time to view it all, let alone go to the cinema.

Finally, the film industry faces the challenge of finding another franchise to rival the extraordinary success of series such as *Harry Potter* or *Lord of the Rings*.

It is a tough call. But one thing is for sure – cinemas will not go with the wind.

Assessing demand for a startup

If your business is a startup, this may well be the trickiest of part of your strategy development. And the most crucial.

Yours may be a new product or service designed to convey a customer benefit not previously realisable. In which case, how do you define the market?

What is market demand for a product that previously has not existed? What is its size? What are its growth prospects?

On the other hand, your startup may be in a market that is already well-defined – like a guest house, which may well be unique and distinctive, but fits snugly into an already buoyant market for three-star tourism in your region.

Or you may be opening a boutique selling designer childrenswear on the high street. Again, that is a definable, existing market to be researched in the same way as set out above.

But what if yours is, indeed, something that has not existed before? How can you convince your backer that there will be buyers of your product or service, and at that price? You need evidence.

You will have to do some test marketing. If yours is a business-to-business proposition, get on the phone and set up meetings with prospective corporate buyers. Explain the benefits of your product and why, at that price, they have a bargain.

Keep a record of these meetings and analyse the findings. Write a report drawing out key conclusions from the discussions, with each supported by bulleted evidence – whether comments from named customers, comments from third parties quoted in the press or data dug up off the web. Collate them into a short and sharp market research report, which will be an appendix to your strategy document.

If yours is a business-to-consumer product or service, test it downtown. Get out your clipboard, stand in a mall or outside a supermarket and talk to shoppers. If you are offering a product, show them; if a service, explain lucidly but swiftly its benefits.

Again, collate the responses, analyse them, draw firm conclusions, support them with quotes and data and stick the market research report in your appendix.

Now, based on those responses, make an estimate of your potential market size. Imagine there were many suppliers of your product or service and that the whole country was aware of its existence, what would the market size be? How does that compare with the market size for products or services not a million miles different from what you will be offering? Does your estimate make sense?

And how about market demand growth? If your startup is serving an existing market, then you can use the same HOOF approach for demand forecasting that an established business would use.

If your startup is for a new market, forecasting demand growth will not be your prime consideration. That will be the existence of such a market in the first place. Any growth on top of discovering and serving a new market will be icing on the cake.

SIMPLE TIP

If your business is a startup, test the market. Pick up the phone or get out and talk to people. Do some primary market research. Amass, digest and analyse pertinent data. Be armed for the inevitable grilling from your backer.

Assessing industry competition

The trouble with the rat race is that even if you win you are still a rat.

Lily Tomlin

Face it. You are not alone. There are others who offer the same, or very similar, products or services as you.

They are your competition. Pay them due respect. Then outwit them.

But, first, think about the issues that apply to all of you, to you and to your competitors. These are the issues of industry competition.

This is the other aspect of understanding the market. The first was the demand side, covered in the last section. This is the supply side. Market demand and industry competition, demand and supply, together compose the market in which your firm operates.

You need to understand both sides of the market in your strategy development.

In this section, we will look at the supply side in five parts:

- Checking out your competitors.
- Gauging competitive intensity.
- Identifying customer buying criteria.
- Deriving factors for success in your industry – a crucial preparatory step prior to creating a competitive advantage for your firm in Part 2.
- Acknowledging competition in a startup.

First, take a good look at your competitors.

Checking out your competitors

With whom do you compete? Do you compete with different firms in your different segments? Do you compete indirectly with other firms?

You need to find out all you can about your competitors, in each segment, whether direct or indirect. Pull together any data, information or opinion you can unearth – from the web, trade fairs, suppliers, customers, industry observers, former employees, etc. – on their sales, sales growth, operating margin (difficult to find if a private company), ownership, segment focus, location of facilities and sales/service teams, physical assets deployed and, of course, strategy – main focus, positioning, USP, pricing policy, recent investment, growth or repositioning plans – the works.

Next, think on this: just how tough is competition in your industry?

SIMPLE TIP

Research your competitors thoroughly. Remember General Sun Tzu's advice: know the enemy.

Gauging competitive intensity

Some industries are more competitive than others. Hopefully, yours is one that is less competitive. But you need to know.

One point of clarification: the term 'industry' sometimes conjures up images such as workers stripped to the waist, toiling to shovel coal into furnaces. Not so here. It is used in its broadest context – any group of producers or service providers collectively serving a market for a particular good or service.

There are six main pressures on any industry (see the following figure) which together act to determine the intensity of competition:

● **Internal rivalry** – from your competitors, depending primarily on how many there are of them, on whether there is a dominant leader, on whether market demand is growing, and on the overall supply–demand balance in the industry; other pressures come from barriers to exit, the existence of which can force players to stay and fight, rather than flee.

● **The threat of new entrants** – which is higher when barriers to entry, whether in capital, technology, operations or personnel, are lower, or when customer switching costs are low.

● **The existence of substitute products or solutions** – which customers could turn to or switch to, thereby abandoning your industry.

● **Environmental factors** – such as government subsidies, regulation, trade unions (where restrictive practices can raise barriers to entry) or law, whether industry, environment, employment or other.

● **Supplier bargaining power** – often a reflection of the numbers of suppliers or the presence of one or two dominant suppliers.

● **Customer bargaining power** – as with supplier power, often dependent on numbers or the extent of dominance by one or two customers.

Five Forces Shaping Competition

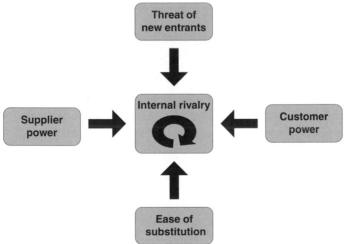

In some industries, such as soft drinks, software and toiletries, these pressures operate benignly to boost profitability – and consistently over the decades. In others, like airlines or textiles, the opposite is true – each of the pressures acts against the players and average profitability over the years is poor.

How tough are each of these pressures in your industry? High, low, medium? Or somewhere in between?

Combine all the pressures and how intense is overall competition in your industry?

Repeat the exercise for each of your main segments. How does competitive intensity differ in each segment?

And what of the future? Is industry competition set to intensify? Because however tough it is at the moment, it results in you and your competitors getting an average operating margin of a certain percent.

But will competitive forces conspire to threaten that margin over the next few years?

If so, you will need to factor that into your strategy development of Part 2.

BLOCKBUSTED

Blockbuster stores were ubiquitous in the early 2000s. From a single store in Dallas in 1985, the company grew to 9,000, employing 60,000 people across the world and with a market cap peaking at $5 billion.

Blockbuster had weathered triumphantly most of the industry pressures it faced:

- **Internal rivalry** – it has seen off or acquired most rivals over the years including its largest competitor, Hollywood Video.

- **The threat of new entrants** – greatly diminished, due to its dominance of the industry.

▶

- **The presence of substitute products or solutions** – a concern, recognised belatedly (see below).

- **Environmental factors** – no significant pressures.

- **Supplier bargaining power** – its dominance enabled it to dictate terms to movie and game suppliers.

- **Customer bargaining power** – customers had the option of mom-and-pop stores or smaller chains, but these did not carry the volumes or range of a Blockbuster store; customers stayed loyal, despite somewhat punitive late return fees.

In 2000, Blockbuster had the opportunity to acquire for $50 million a startup online DVD subscription postal operator with a nascent streaming service. It opted instead to develop its own offering, albeit four years behind. Netflix now has a market cap of over $60 billion.

One industry pressure alone had been sufficient to scupper Blockbuster – the substitute solution. The alternative offering of Netflix, likewise of Hulu, proved such a disruptor that the blocks and mortar movie rental store was busted.

Identifying customer buying criteria

'All business success rests on something labelled a sale, which at least momentarily weds company and customer,' wrote Tom Peters.

But why does that customer buy from that company? That is the question.

What do customers in one of your main segments need from you and your competitors? Are they looking for the lowest possible price for a given level of product (or service)? The highest quality product irrespective of price? Or something in between?

Do customers have the same needs in your other business segments? Do some customer groups place greater importance on certain needs?

What exactly do they want in terms of product? The highest specifications? Fastest delivery? The most reliable? The best technical back-up? The most sympathetic customer service?

SIMPLE TIP

All this is very well in theory, you may ask, but how do you know what customers want? Simple. Ask them!

It does not take long. You would be surprised how, after just a few discussions with customers from any one group, a predictable pattern begins to emerge. Some may consider one need 'very important', others just 'important'.

But it is unlikely that another will say that it is 'unimportant'. Customers in any one group tend to have similar needs.

Customer needs from their suppliers are called customer buying criteria and usefully can be grouped into six categories. They are customer needs relating to the following:

- **effectiveness** of the product (or service) in terms, for example, of quality, design, features, specifications, functionality, reliability;
- **efficiency** of the service, getting it to the customer conveniently and on time;
- **range** of products (or services) provided;
- **relationship** with the producer;
- **premises** (applicable only if the customer needs to visit the supplier's premises);
- **price**, which tends to be a more important criterion the less essential the product (or service).

They can be remembered conveniently with, perhaps, droid-like undertones, as the *E2-R2-P2* of customer buying criteria – see the following figure.

The E2-P2-R2 of customer buying criteria

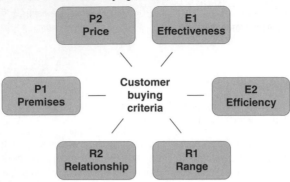

Which of these criteria are most important to your customers? How does importance differ in each of your main segments? Are any likely to become more or less important over time?

Once you have identified these customer buying criteria, and their relative levels of importance, you will be able move on to the next challenge – what your firm and your competitors need to do to successfully meet these criteria.

SIMPLE TIP

Some customers may have a hidden agenda. They see a customer survey meeting as an opportunity to get you to nudge down your prices. Or improve your service offering, incurring extra cost, without increasing pricing. They may rate price as a most important criterion even though they are concerned primarily with product quality.

Bear this in mind. It is business – and human nature. Such hidden agendas do not negate the validity of the customer survey, but judgement is required.

Deriving factors for success

What do firms in your industry need to do to succeed? What factors are key to success?

What do you need to get right to satisfy customer buying criteria *and* run a sound business?

Such factors may be product (or service) quality, consistency, availability, range and product development (R&D). On the service side, factors can include distribution capability, sales and marketing effectiveness, customer service and post-sale technical support.

Other factors relate to the cost side of things, such as location of premises, scale of operations, state-of-the-art, cost-effective equipment and operational process efficiency.

To identify which are the most important factors for success in each of your main business segments, you need to undertake these steps:

- Identify factors needed to meet buying criteria.
- Assess management and market share.
- Rate these factors for importance.
- Identify any must-haves.

Let us look briefly at each of these steps.

Identify factors needed to meet buying criteria

Here you convert the customer buying criteria you identified above into factors for success. In other words, you work out *what your business has to do to meet your customer's needs*.

These factors often can be the flipside to customer buying criteria. The customer may seek product functionality, so research and development will be a factor for success. The customer may seek product reliability, so quality control will be a factor for success. Delivery to schedule may be a customer buying criterion, so spare capacity and/or manufacturing efficiency may be a factor for success. These are factors in which you can differentiate your product or service from the competition – known rather ungainly as differentiation-related success factors.

There is one customer buying criterion that needs special attention and that is price. Customers of most services expect a keen *price*. Producers need to keep their *costs* down. Price is a customer buying criterion, cost competitiveness a factor for success.

Determinants of cost competitiveness in your business could include location of facilities, cost of materials, operational efficiency, use of subcontractors, outsourcing of business processes, overhead control, remuneration levels and IT systems. These are cost-related success factors.

And size may be important. Other things being equal, the larger the business the lower costs should be *for each unit* of business sold. These are 'economies of scale' and may apply not just to the unit cost of materials or other variable costs, where a larger business will benefit from negotiated volume discounts, but also to overheads, such as marketing, where the same expense on, for example, a magazine advertisement or a trade show stand can be spread over a larger revenue volume base.

Assess management and market share

We have derived two sets of factors from the customer buying criteria set out above: differentiation-related and cost-related. There are two more specific factors to be considered: management and market share.

How important is management in general in your industry? Think on whether a well-managed company, with a superb sales and marketing team reinforced by an efficient operations team, but with an average product, would outperform a poorly managed company with a superb product in your industry.

There is one final factor – an important one – that we need to take into account that is not directly derived from customer buying criteria: market share. The larger the market share, the stronger, typically, the provider.

A high market share can manifest itself in a number of different competitive advantages. One such area is in lower unit costs, but we have already covered this under economies of scale, so we must be careful not to double count.

Market share is an indicator of the breadth and depth of your customer relationships and your business reputation. Since it is more difficult to gain a new customer than to do repeat business with an existing customer, the provider with the larger market share typically has a competitive advantage – *the power of the incumbent*.

The power of the incumbent rises in proportion to the switching costs – not just the financial costs of switching, but the time, hassle and even emotional costs. It is less of a wrench to change your printer than your accountant.

Rate these factors for importance

You have set out which are the most important factors for success in your business. But just how important are they, one with another? Run through each one and assign a rating: is it of high importance, medium or low? Or somewhere in between?

You may prefer, like me, to use a simple quantitative approach. You can give a weight, to the nearest 5 or 10 per cent, as to the relative importance of each factor and juggle around with the weights until you have a realistic allocation which, crucially, tots up to 100 per cent.

The great advantage of a quantitative approach is that you will be able to deploy a simple Excel chart in Part 2 to derive a rating of the overall competitive position of your business. This can then be compared with ratings over time and with those of your competitors.

But, in the interests of keeping strategy plain and simple, and appreciating that not every reader feels comfortable with a quantitative approach, rest assured that rating factors in words, such as of high or low importance, can work just as well.

The next figure shows an example of the factors for success identified in a niche engineering market, which I worked on a few years ago. The factors are rated for importance in words (column 2) and then in numbers (column 3). The choice is yours.

Factors for success: an example

Factors for success in engineering niche market	Importance	Weight
Market share	*Med/high*	15%
Cost factors	*Very high*	35%
Differentiation factors:		
Product capability and range	*Med/high*	15%
Product reliability	*Med/high*	15%
Engineering service network	*Med*	10%
Customer service	*Med*	10%
Total weighting		**100%**

Identify any must-haves

There is one final wrinkle. But it may be crucial.

Is one of the success factors in your business so important that if you do not rank highly against it you should not even be in business? You simply will not begin to compete, let alone succeed? You will not win any business or you will not be able to deliver on the business you win? In other words, it is a *must-have* factor, rather than a mere *should-have*.

Must a business in your marketplace have, for example, the right ISO classification to win future orders in a competitively intensifying environment? Must a provider of your service have a specific degree or qualification before being able to attract a single customer?

Are any of the factors for success in your industry must-haves? You will need to bear this in mind when assessing your firm's competitive position in Part 2.

SIMPLE TIP

Do not end up with too many factors for success or you may lose the wood for the trees. Market share, management, two or three cost-related factors and five or six differentiation-related factors should be fine – a total of ten or so.

A SORRY AFFAIR

In the early 2010s, a Canada-based global dating agency site was riding high. It seemed to have a winning formula. It was outrageous, even immoral, many argued, and its controversy continually propelled its fame, or infamy, thereby driving rapid revenue growth at relatively modest marketing spend – a big bang for the buck, so to speak.

In mid-2015, all went horribly wrong. The agency got the one thing wrong that, above all else, it should have got right, the one success factor that was critical to being in the game. This was not just an ordinary, should-have 'ranking' success factor, but a must-have, 'screening' factor. It was confidentiality . . .

The agency's IT security systems proved inadequate and its customer database was hacked – including names, home addresses, emails, credit card information and sexual preferences. The hackers threatened to release the data unless the agency closed down, permanently. The agency held out, the data went public and all hell broke loose.

Why should that be the end of the world, you might think? Hacks and leaks are happening everywhere these days, even into the databases of major political parties. Millions of people sign up to dating agencies, online or offline, so, if personal information went public, why should that be so disastrous?

Because Ashley Madison was an adultery website, that is why. Its strapline was 'Life is short. Have an affair!' Anyone's name appearing on that

▶

site would display, at the least, that person's intentions. The implications of exposure could be professional ridicule, marital disharmony or worse.

Ashley Madison failed to meet a 'screening' success factor. With its inadequate IT infrastructure, it should not have been in business. The leaks also showed that it was an agency deficient in another 'ranking' success factor: integrity. It turned out that tens of thousands of its female members were non-existent phantoms, so-called 'fem-bots', planted there by its employees to titillate the overwhelmingly male paid-up membership. It also transpired that members keen to quit and who had paid a 'full delete' option to get rid of all traces of their personal details were still sitting there on the Ashley Madison files.

Ashley Madison claims to have learnt its lesson. It has invested heavily in strengthening its IT systems, has banned the creation of fembots and has relaunched under the strapline 'Find your moment'. But the episode was costly. The agency lost a fifth of its $100 million revenues and two fifths of its profits in 2016. A company valued by its former CEO at $1 billion is now facing a class action lawsuit from aggrieved former members totalling in the hundreds of millions of dollars.

Ashley Madison had an affair, though not one of its choosing.

Acknowledging competition in a startup

Too many startup business plans are based on the premise that theirs is a new, revolutionary concept. Competition is non-existent or irrelevant.

In the vast majority of cases, this presumption is both wrong and dangerous. At best, it is only ever partially true.

There is always competition. Whatever is your solution to the perceived needs of the customer, someone else somewhere else has another solution. Or will have. If they do not have a solution now, they may well do once they have seen yours.

So you need to look at three aspects of competition in a startup:

- Direct competition.
- Indirect competition.
- Competitive response.

Direct competition

If your new venture is a business with a clearly defined existing marketplace, then your analysis of industry competition will be no different from that of an established business.

You will identify the competitors, soon to be augmented by one, and assess competitive intensity, soon to be intensified, perhaps, by your firm's entry.

An example, as introduced in the section on market demand, would be a startup boutique specialising in designer childrenswear. Your competitors would include other such boutiques, any boutiques focusing on adult clothes but also offering a selection for children, childrenswear chainstores, the childrenswear departments of department stores and all of these variants using alternative routes to market, such as catalogue shopping or the internet.

You will be entering a highly competitive market – retail can be an unforgivingly competitive arena – but, hopefully, with a distinctive edge that you will set out forcefully in Part 2.

Indirect competition

What if your idea is a genuinely new concept? Who are your competitors?

They are whoever was providing an alternative solution to the customer before your business existed, competing for a similar share of the customer's wallet as you are.

Suppose you invented an ingenious wooden rollerball back massaging device that released aromatherapy oils as you massaged. It is new, it is unique, it is brilliant, it works!

But it has competition. The customer's need is relief from back tension or discomfort. The customer is prepared to dip into their pocket to relieve that pain.

The customer has a range of alternative solutions – other wooden rollerball devices, plastic and metal versions, electrically powered massage devices, massage chairs. They can go to a masseur, even an aromatherapist. They can purchase the oils and self-administer. They can take pills.

All these are competitors, even if only indirect ones. Yours will occupy a particular price positioning – above basic rollerball devices, below power-driven ones – but the customer has the option to trade up or down.

In the next part, you will consider the pros and cons of alternative solutions. You will lay out your stall. But it is a stall in relation to the alternative providers – and these competitors need to be identified in this section and the intensity of this competition assessed.

Competitive response

What will be the reaction of competitors, direct and indirect, if your venture turns out to be a success?

You cannot assume that they will stand idly by and cheer you on.

If your new concept is patent protected, that is great. But could there be ways for a nimble competitor to negotiate a path around the patent, and legally? Offering a slight variant on the theme often can be enough.

And how will you respond, not if but when your competitors respond to your market entry?

SIMPLE TIP

If your firm fares well, it will ring a bell – for the competitor as for the customer.

Suppose your childrenswear boutique is successful. How will the department store down the road respond? Perhaps by cordoning off the childrenswear department, refitting it with a whacky, kiddie-enthralling décor – or even engaging a clown every Saturday morning? How would you respond to that response?

Suppose your oil-infused rollerball massaging device was successful? How will producers of basic devices respond? Will they copy the device if it is unpatented? If patented, could they offer their devices along with freestanding oils for self-administering at 15 per cent below your price? How would you respond to that?

Consider competitive response. And prepare your retaliatory response to that response.

To summarise the main points of this section, you will by now have confirmed, let us hope, that your firm is operating in a market where, in its main segments:

- Market demand is sizeable and growing.
- Industry competition is manageable.
- Demand will continue to exceed supply.

Next we look at your firm – how it is positioned in this market and how it can develop a sustainable competitive advantage.

2
Creating competitive advantage

If you don't have a competitive advantage, don't compete.

Jack Welch

- Tracking your competitive position
- Targeting the strategic gap
- Bridging the gap: business strategy
- Bridging the gap: corporate strategy

You have built the foundation for your strategy development. You understand the market and where it is heading. Now you need to place your firm within that context.

You need to track your competitive position over time and pinpoint your competitive advantage. Then you should raise your sights. Figure out what the strategic gap is between the capabilities of your business now and where you would want them to be in the future.

Finally, you assess the ways in which you can bridge that gap. That is how you are going to create a sustainable competitive advantage.

We start with tracking competitive position.

Tracking your competitive position

Big will not beat small anymore. It will be the fast beating the slow.

Rupert Murdoch

You need to set out your firm's competitive position and pinpoint your competitive advantage – for each main business segment. You should track it over time – and do likewise for each of your main competitors.

This applies whether yours is an established business or a startup.

Competitive position in an established business

In Part 1, you identified the key factors needed for success in your main business segments over the next few years. And you rated each by level of importance – or, if you were mathematically inclined, with a percentage weighting.

How does your firm rate against each of those success factors?

How do your principal competitors rate?

What is your overall competitive position in each main segment? And theirs? How do your relative positions differ by segment?

You need to rate your competitive position, and that of each principal competitor, over time and for each main segment.

You could do this right now, at your desk, based on feedback you and your sales and purchasing teams have received from customers and suppliers over the years. Or you could do it more methodically, via a structured interviewing programme with selected customers, ex-customers, potential customers, suppliers, competitors and other industry observers.

Keep the interviewing upbeat and positive. Make sure the interviewee is left feeling that both parties have gained from the discussion and that time has not been wasted.

You will assess your strengths and weaknesses and those of your peers. It will pinpoint your sources of competitive advantage – as well as those of your most formidable competitors.

The process of rating competitive position is straightforward: a 0–5 rating system works best. If your business performs about the same as your peers against a success factor, give yourself a score in the middle, a 3 (*good, favourable*). If you perform very strongly, even dominantly, give it a 5 (*very strong*). Poorly, a 1 (*weak*). If you perform not quite as well as most others, give yourself a 2 (*tenable*). Better than most, a 4 (*strong*).

Now do the same for each of your principal competitors against that success factor. Who is the best performer against this factor? Does the company merit a 5, or are they better but not *that* much better than others, and deserve a 4?

And so on against each success factor.

Arrange the information in a table:

- Factors for success in column 1.
- Level of importance in column 2, in either words or symbols (if you are using MS Word) or percentage weighting (if MS Excel).
- Your firm's rating in column 3.
- The ratings of each main competitor in columns 4 and 5, or more.

If you have used Excel, your competitive position will fall out at the bottom of the spreadsheet. If you prefer to stay in Word, you will need to eyeball the ratings alongside the relative importance of each and form your overall conclusion. You will not be far out.

The following figure gives an example, taken from a recent strategy assignment. It shows that the company was the leading player in its niche engineering market, with a competitive position significantly above those of its two main competitors. But there was no room for complacency. Though the company had the largest presence in the market, the best engineering service network and a strong cost base, competitor A had developed a product with enhanced features and functionality that was proving attractive to customers. Competitor B, meanwhile, had a competitive cost base, but was still some way behind in both product and service capabilities.

Competitive position: an example

Factors for success in engineering niche market	*Importance*	The company	Competitor A	Competitor B
Market share	*Med/high*	5	3.5	2
Cost factors	*Very high*	4	3.5	4.5
Differentiation factors:				
Product capability and range	*Med/high*	4	4.5	3
Product reliability	*Med/high*	4	4	2.5
Engineering service network	*Med*	5	3.5	2.5
Customer service	*Med*	3	3	2
Overall competitive position		**4+**	**3.5+**	**3+**

Key: 1 = Weak, 2 = Tenable, 3 = Favourable, 4 = Strong, 5 = Dominant

Overall, the company had the strongest competitive position, with a rating of roughly 4+, compared with its two main rivals' ratings of 3.5+ and 3+. Note that these overall ratings were derived from eyeballing ratings against each factor against the relative importance of the factor – not a scientific approach, but one that is very much preferable to using no weighting at all.

Better, though, to use indicative percentage weightings for each success factor and leave it to Excel to derive the exact competitive position. Using the percentage weightings in 'Factors for success: an example', on page 60 the company's competitive position emerged as 4.2, compared to its main rival's 3.7.

Competing by segment

Apply the same process for each of your main segments. You will find that your competitive position may well differ from segment to segment. This may be because one success factor in which you are particularly strong (or weak) has a lesser importance in one segment than another.

Or it may be that you are simply stronger in one segment than another. For instance, your business may have an enviable track record in service and repair in one segment, but you have not long been in another – rating a 5 in the first, but only a 2 in the other.

Competing over time

So far your analysis of competitive position has been static. You have rated your firm's current competitiveness and those of others. But that is only the first part of the story. How has your competitive position changed over the last few years and how is it likely to change over the next few years? You need to understand the dynamics. Is it set to improve or worsen?

The simplest way to do this is to add an extra column to your chart, representing your position in, say, three years' time. Then you can build in any improvements in your ratings against each success factor. These prospective improvements need, for the time being, to be both in the pipeline *and* likely. In the next section, we shall assess how you can *proactively and systematically* improve your competitive position. That is strategy. But, for now, it is useful to see how your competitive position seems set to evolve naturally over the next few years, assuming no significant change in strategy.

Remember, however, that improved competitive position is a two-edged sword. Your competitors, too, will have plans. This is where analysis of competitive dynamics gets challenging. It is easy enough to know what you are planning but what are your competitors up to?

Try adding a couple of further columns representing your two most fearsome competitors as they may be in three years' time. Do you have any idea what they are planning to do to improve their competitiveness in the near future? What are they likely to do? What could they do? *What are you afraid they will do?*

Returning to the example of the UK niche engineering company, management was aware that competitor A had plans to outsource certain components and reduce cost and set up a joint venture to enhance its engineering service capability. Competitor A's strategy seemed set to narrow the competitive gap unless my client deployed a proactive strategy focusing on R&D – see the figure below.

Future competitive position: an example

Factors for success in engineering niche market	*Importance*	The company	Competitor A	Competitor A tomorrow
Market share	*Med/high*	5	3.5	4
Cost factors	*Very high*	4	3.5	4
Differentiation factors:				
Product capability and range	*Med/high*	4	4.5	4.5
Product reliability	*Med/high*	4	4	4
Engineering service network	*Med*	5	3.5	4
Customer service	*Med*	3	3	3.5
Overall competitive position		**4+**	**3.5+**	**4+**

Key: 1 = Weak, 2 = Tenable, 3 = Favourable, 4 = Strong, 5 = Dominant

Getting past first base

In the last section, we introduced the concept of the must-have success factor – without a good rating in which your business cannot even begin to compete.

Did you find a must-have factor in any of your business segments? If so, how do you rate against it? Favourable, strong? Fine. OK-ish? Questionable. Weak? Troublesome. A straight zero, not even a 1? You are out. You do not get past first base.

And what about in a few years' time? Could any success factor develop into a must-have? How will you rate then? Will you get past first base?

And, even though you rate as tenable against a must-have factor today, might it slip over time? Could it slide below 2, into tricky territory?

This may be a case of being cruel to be kind. It is better to know. The sooner you realise that you are in a wrong segment, the sooner you can withdraw and focus resources on the right segments.

Implications for future market share

This competitive position analysis plays a useful role in business planning. It gives you an idea of how your firm is likely to fare over the next few years *in relation to the market as a whole*.

If your overall competitive position turns out to be around 3, or good/favourable, you should, other things being equal, be able to grow business *in line with the market* over the next few years. In other words, to hold market share.

If it is around 4 or above, you should be able to *beat the market*, to gain market share, again, other things being equal. Suppose you forecast market demand growth of 10 per cent a year in Part 1. With a strong competitive position, rated at around 4, you should feel comfortable that you can grow your business at, say, 12–15 per cent a year.

If your competitive position is around 2, however, you will be less confident about your business prospects. It is more likely that you will *underperform the market* and, if your boss is expecting the firm to outpace the market, something will have to change!

Implications for strategy development

Competitive position analysis also throws up some facts and judgements highly useful for strategy development:

● How you compete overall in key segments – hence where you are most likely to be most profitable relative to the competition.

- Areas of strength in key segments, which can be built on.

- Areas of weakness in some segments, which may need to be worked on.

- Areas of strength or weakness common to many or all segments, which could well be a priority to build or work on.

- Relative competitiveness in each key segment.

- Change in competitiveness over time.

In summary, your source of competitive advantage, tracked over time.

It will form the basis for identification of the strategic gap in the next section.

SIMPLE TIP

Too much analysis hinders decision making – do not do this competitive position analysis for too many segments, too many success factors, too many competitors or too many years, past and future. Keep it simple – opt for the main segments, the main success factors, the main competitors, now and three years' hence; look for the main findings, the key lessons; drill down further only if necessary and potentially illuminating.

WORK OUT AND PARTAY?!

I do not get gyms. Why go through all the grief of running, lifting or pulling stuck inside a claustrophobic box when you could be doing the same thing in the park, breathing in the fresh air?

But were I a generation younger, Gymbox might have tempted me. Its USP is to make gym work party-time. That sounds more like it . . .

Two directly contrasting health and fitness trends have been occurring in the UK in the twenty-first century. At one end of the scale, people have become increasingly sedentary and overweight. Obesity levels have risen from 1 in 65 in the 1960s to an astonishing 1 in 4. At the other end

▶

of the scale, many are obsessing about getting fitter, firmer, more 'ripped'.

Membership of fitness clubs or gyms has grown at an average 3.5 per cent/year since 2008. There are now over 9 million members, 1 in every 7 people in the UK – lower than penetration rates in Germany or Scandinavia (1 in 5), but higher than pre-crash.

Overall demand growth masks a veritable revolution within the industry. Low-cost entrants, led by Pure Gym and The Gym Group, later joined by the even lower-cost easyGym and Sports Direct Fitness, have driven member growth, pulling in new gym-goers but also poaching from existing players. Pure Gym has already become the largest player in terms of members. Upmarket chains like Virgin Active and David Lloyd have consolidated, while mid-range players have struggled – with LA Fitness exiting the market, their sites snapped up by the no-frills players – no pools, no saunas, no cafés, no towels, no contracts – and open 24/7.

The fitness industry has headed in the direction of the airlines and, yet, more akin perhaps to the hotels sector, which also attracted a wave of low-cost entrants, opportunities for competitive advantage based on niche differentiation have also sprung up.

You want to work out under the guidance not just of a trainer but a DJ? That's Gymbox – 'We were young, hungry and buff, no fans of the bland, beige and boringly snooty health clubs'. Gymbox threw in exciting new products, too, with boxing rings, combat cages and aerial hoops – 'we love being the fitness industry's version of Marmite'.

Gymbox took the opposite route to the low-cost entrants, a highly differentiated – and by no means cheap – route. It worked. By 2016, it was turning over £16 million with an EBITDA margin of 34 per cent and had raised a further £40 million for expansion.

It is not alone. Other fitness entrants have differentiated and prospered: Frame specifically targets female gym-goers, with its 'feel-good, energetic and fun-filled classes' and members are encouraged to linger in the Frame Café and the Frame Shop; Fierce Grace helps practitioners achieve 'the ultimate blend of strength and flexibility for both body and mind' through its own variant on Hot Yoga; and, further afield, Brooklyn Zoo in New York, with its multiple levels of structures to jump and climb on – some up to 20 feet high, a vast dance floor and a massive trampoline, offers a workout via the esoteric sport of parkour.

This is gym blending with extreme sport – differentiation in the extreme.

Competitive position for a startup

The process set out in this section is not that different for a startup, whether serving an existing market or creating a new one. You need to assess your likely competitive position in the main segments where you intend to compete and develop a strategy to enhance that competitiveness over time.

There are three main differences:

- Your competitive position is in the future rather than the present tense.
- It will be affected adversely from the outset by a low rating against all success factors pertaining to experience.
- You must, nevertheless, have some evident competitive advantage just to survive in the early years.

Your competitive position in a new venture is a judgement more on the immediate future than the present. For an established business, the debate revolves as much around the present and recent past as it does the future – around the weighting of success factors and/or your ratings against them, as justified by evidence from customer, supplier and other interviews, each of which will be as much based on fact and performance track record as judgement.

But, for a startup, the debate will be part conjecture, especially if your venture is to a new market. There is no track record of your performance, nor maybe on the market. For the latter, though, you must find evidence from any which source – see Part 1.

There is little you can do about your new venture's rating against those suc- cess factors that demand experience – unless, for example, you find an expe- rienced ally. Thus your rating against market share will be low at the outset, so too, perhaps, against some cost-related factors, especially those relating to scale.

Likewise, your rating against some differentiation factors may be low. Your lack of track record may count against you in consistency of product quality, delivery, customer service or sales and marketing.

In that case, how will your firm compete? The answer is that it is not easy being a new entrant in an existing market. Your competitive position will, indeed, be low, relative to the leaders at the outset. But, if you are addressing a growing market and/or you can differentiate your product or service suffi- ciently, things should improve. Your competitive position in three to five years' time should have improved measurably – your market share rating should be up, your unit costs down, your service performance improved.

But this analysis further highlights the importance of segmentation. If your new venture does not serve an existing market but creates its own, then all changes. The analysis of competition will be undertaken not for the market as a whole but for your addressed product/market segment. And, if that is a new segment, created by your new venture, effectively you have no *direct* competition.

But there are two caveats:

- You will have indirect competition, as discussed in Part 1, who may up their game if you are successful.
- You will, in time, face competition from new entrants, if your new market is worthy of pursuit.

To survive the hostile early years of a startup, you must create a distinct competitive advantage. This can take a multitude of forms, including most commonly:

- a new product (or service);
- a similar product but at lower cost;

- a similar product but with a distinct element of differentiation, whether in quality (features, functionality, reliability?), distribution (electronic rather than physical?), delivery, service (pre-sale help, after-sale care?), marketing (a theme that resonates?);

- a similar product tailored to a new market;

- a similar product offered to a new region.

Whatever your source of perceived competitive advantage, it must carry enough weight to give your new business at least a tenable competitive position in those early years of the venture.

If your venture manages no more than a rating of 1 (out of 5) for market share, as is likely, 1.5 for cost factors, also likely in the early days, 2 for product quality, 2 for service and 2 for delivery, that will give you a startup competitive position well below 2, depending on success factor weightings.

That is untenable. Your startup has no distinct competitive advantage. It will fail.

If, however, you manage to earn a rating of 4, even 5, against a couple of those success factors, in those specific areas of your competitive advantage, your initial competitive position may emerge closer to 2.5 or 3 – which is not too bad for a startup, given the inevitably low ratings against market share, scale-based cost factors and management in the early days. It is a tenable, bordering on favourable, competitive position.

The key to a successful startup, to repeat, is competitive advantage.

For further reading on competitive advantage in a startup, try John Mullins' *The New Business Road Test*. This is essential reading on the preparatory work and research you should undertake before firming up a strategy for a startup, especially in a new market.

OF DAMES AND DETECTIVES

I always enjoy reading about a small company that has made it. By making it, I am not talking about some inter-galactic entrepreneur doing an Apple or a Virgin. But an entrepreneur following a dream, surviving

▶

through the ups and downs and earning enough for a comfortable life-style for the family.

The vast majority of businesses are small businesses. And it is always sad to hear of one going under. Each founder has shown such spirit, such initiative, such courage to set out on his or her own that few merit such a fate.

But often the failure of a small business comes about because it does not possess a sustainable competitive advantage. It is, in effect, a me-too business. It is living on borrowed time.

Here is my favourite example of a business with a sustainable competitive advantage – fictional, but no less instructive for that.

The No. 1 Ladies Detective Agency was launched by Alexander McCall Smith's wonderfully warm, wise and witty creation, Mma Precious Ramotswe, in downtown Gaborone, the capital of Botswana. She captures business through being the first and only female detective agency in town – an initial competitive advantage, yet sustainable in that, even if a direct competitor were to emerge, Mma Ramotswe's would remain forever the first, hence the No. 1 Ladies Detective Agency.

What is your firm's competitive advantage? Is it sustainable?

Targeting the strategic gap

We know what we are, but know not what we may be.

William Shakespeare

You have worked out the current competitiveness of your business. Where do you want it to be in three to five years' time? What is your target competitive position?

You need to identify the strategic gap between where you are now and where the ideal player is, now and in the future. You will then set your sights on the extent to which you aim to narrow, even bridge, that gap.

There are two distinct types of gap:

- **The portfolio gap** – in which segments you should compete.
- **The capability gap** – how well you compete in each segment.

The portfolio and capability gaps together form the strategic gap. Here you will identify and target the gap. In this section you will look at the strategic options for bridging it.

Targeting the portfolio gap

Where should your business compete? In which segments? How can you enhance the strategic position of your business?

What should your portfolio of business segments look like? What is the gap from today's portfolio?

The attractiveness/advantage matrix, an invaluable business tool, should reveal all. It will show how competitive your business is in segments assessed in terms of market attractiveness. Ideally, you should invest in segments where you are strongest and/or that are the most attractive. And you should consider withdrawal from segments where you are weaker and/or where your competitive position is untenable.

And perhaps you should be looking to enter another business segment (or segments) in *more* attractive markets than the ones you currently address? If so, do you have grounds for believing that you would be at least reasonably placed in this new segment? And that soon you could become well placed?

First, you need to specify how to define an 'attractive' market segment. This is, to some extent, sector-specific and no two strategists will come up with the same list but, over the years, I have found these five factors to be both pertinent and relatively measurable in most sectors:

- Market size.
- Market demand growth.
- Competitive intensity.
- Industry profitability.
- Market risk – cyclicality, volatility (for example, exposure to country risk).

The larger the market and the faster it is growing, the more attractive, other things being equal, is the market. Likewise, the greater the industry profitability. But be careful with the other two factors, where the converse applies. The *greater* the competitive intensity and the *greater* its risk, the *less* attractive is the market.

An example may help (see the following figure). Suppose your business is in four segments and you are contemplating entering a fifth. You rate each of the segments against each of the criteria for market attractiveness. You take an average, simple in this case but it could be weighted, to arrive at a measure of overall attractiveness. Segment D emerges as the most attractive, followed by new segment E. B is rather unattractive.

Market attractiveness: an example

Segments:	A	B	C	D	E (new)
Market size	3	2	2	3	3
Market growth	1	2	3	5	5
Competitive intensity	2	2	3	4	5
Industry profitability	3	3	4	2	2
Market risk	5	2	4	4	2
Overall attractiveness	**2.8**	**2.2**	**3.2**	**3.6**	**3.4**

Key to rating: 1 = Unattractive, 3 = Reasonably attractive, 5 = Highly attractive (For competitive intensity, remember that the more intense the competition, the *less* attractive the market. Likewise, for market risk: the riskier the market, the *less* attractive.)

Next, you pull out the ratings of competitive position you undertook in the last section, for each segment (for example the figure 'Competitive position: an example' on page 39). Now you can draw up the attractiveness/advantage matrix by placing each segment in the appropriate part of the matrix (see the following figure). Segment A, for example, has a competitive position rating of 4 (out of 5) and a market attractiveness rating of 2.8 (also out of 5).

The segment's position in the chart will reflect both its competitive position (along the x-axis) and its market attractiveness (along the y-axis). The size of each circle should be roughly proportional to the segment's contribution to operating profit.

The closer your segment is positioned towards the top right-hand corner, the better placed it is. Above the top right dotted diagonal, you should invest further in that segment, building on your advantage. Should the segment sink below the bottom left dotted diagonal, however, you should harvest the

Strategic position: an example

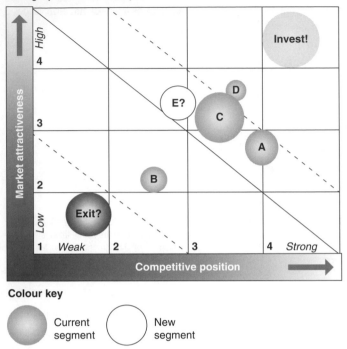

Colour key

Current segment   New segment

Note: Diameter of bubble proportional to profit (except for segment E)
Source: General Electric, McKinsey & Co. and various

business for cash or consider withdrawal. Segments placed along the main diagonal are reasonably placed and should be held, with investment cases carefully scrutinised.

The overall strategic position shown in the example seems sound. It shows favourable strength in the biggest and reasonably attractive segment C, and an excellent position in the somewhat less attractive segment A. Segment D is highly promising and demands more attention, given the currently low level of profit.

Segment B should, perhaps, be exited – it is a rather unattractive segment and your firm is not that well placed. The new segment E seems promising.

You may consider the following strategic options worthy of further analysis:

- Holding and steady development in segments A and C.
- Investment in segment D.
- Entry to segment E (with competitive position improving over time as market share develops).
- Harvesting or exit from segment B.

How is the overall strategic position in your business? Hopefully, your *main* segments, from which you derive most revenues, should find themselves positioned above the main diagonal.

Do you have any new segments in mind? How attractive are they? How well placed would you be?

Are there any segments you should be thinking of getting out of? Be careful here, though. Would withdrawal from one segment adversely affect your position in another? Might it be better to persevere with a loss leader?

Which segments are so important that you would derive greatest benefit from improving your competitive position? Where should you concentrate your efforts?

SIMPLE TIP

A major criticism of this portfolio planning tool lies in its subjectivity. Some argue that so many judgement calls are made throughout the process that deriving strategy from its findings is fraught with danger.

But strategy is all about judgement, albeit backed up by fact where available. The very process of constructing the matrix, taking in work done earlier, is illuminating, instructive and crucial to strategy development. It forces you to think about what drives success in your business, how your business fares against those drivers and what you need to do to fare better in the future. It is not only a portfolio planning tool, but the first step in identifying the strategic gap.

No strategy tools can obviate the need for judgement. Nor should they be expected to.

Targeting the capability gap

You have targeted the portfolio gap. Next up is the capability gap.

Targeting the capability gap can be undertaken in four stages:

1   Envision future scenarios.

2   Profile the ideal player.

3   Stretch your sights.

4   Specify the capability gap.

Start with the crystal ball.

1 Envision future scenarios

Try envisioning the future of your marketplace. Will it be more competitive? Will customers have different expectations? Will players need to develop different capabilities?

Try thinking 'out of the box', using the imagination, stimulating the right side of the brain. Try brainstorming.

Try to develop a range of scenarios on what may happen in your marketplace. Venture beyond the more likely outcomes – you have already drawn those up. Think of those that are less expected but still *quite* likely to occur. Stay clear of fanciful outcomes with only a remote chance of happening. Go for scenarios that could actually happen.

Under such scenarios, will customer needs and buying criteria change? Which success factors will become more prominent? Which less so?

2 Profile the ideal player

We can define the ideal player in your marketplace as the one who would achieve the highest possible rating against each of the success factors identified – whether those of today or those that you have identified as becoming more prominent in the future.

How close to becoming this ideal player should you aim?

3 Stretch your sights

What is the gap between your firm's capabilities now and those to which you aspire? Should you reconsider where you aim to be? Are you sure you have set sufficiently challenging goals?

Should you be stretching your sights?

Where do you want to be in tomorrow's marketplace? Do you want to become a good player in tomorrow's marketplace? A strong player?

Or do you want to *lead* in tomorrow's marketplace?

Do you want to get as far as you can towards becoming the Ideal Player of Tomorrow? Do you want to go for goal? (See the following figure.)

Going for goal

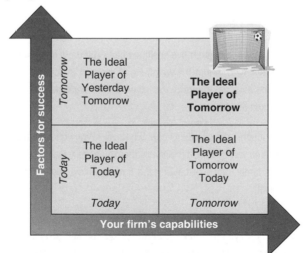

If so, remember that the goalposts may well have shifted by the time you are ready to shoot. Time moves on and the ideal player, in five years' time, will have a different mix of capabilities to the equivalent today. Perhaps only with slight differences in nuance, perhaps radically different.

The *Going for goal* chart highlights three important points:

- It is fine being the *Ideal Player of Today*, but today lasts only one day.
- If your firm does not develop the extra capabilities required to meet the customer needs of tomorrow, you will become the *Ideal Player of Yesterday Tomorrow*.
- There is little point in developing extra capabilities today, unless customers need them, or you will become the *Ideal Player of Tomorrow Today*.

Once you have raised your sights, perhaps to the very top, you need to specify the capability gap and, in the next section, plan how you are going to bridge it.

4 Specify the capability gap

You need to revisit the competitive position charts you drew up earlier. Check for any changes over time in the weighting of success factors as a result of changes in the external marketplace, given the scenario development you have undertaken above.

You can now identify the capability gap. Whatever rating you have given your business in three years' time, it is unlikely that you have arrived at a 5 against each success factor. Any shortfall below a 5 represents a capability gap with the ideal player.

But is it reasonable to believe you could achieve a 5 in each success factor over the next few years? Unlikely. Better to set yourself a realistic target, albeit one that is stretched and challenging. Against which factor should you be raising your game? And by how much?

You now target that gap. Often that means just the insertion of an active verb, such as 'improve'. You have found a capability gap in your distribution – targeting that gap means improving distribution.

Sometimes, targeting the gap requires further thought. The capability gap may be too broad and you might consider exiting the segment.

Let us return to the example we used earlier in this section of the business operating in four main segments and contemplating entry to another. As a result of profiling the ideal player and raising sights, the CEO might now target the capability gap as follows:

- Improve margin in segment A.
- Withdraw in segment B, recognising an unbridgeable gap.
- Improve distribution In segment C.
- Improve product speed to market in segment D.
- Enter segment E.
- Lower production costs across all segments.
- Improve enterprise resource management (ERM) systems across the business.

The impact of this targeting of the capability gap could be as shown in the following figure. The competitive position of each segment, especially E, should be improved, other than B, which will be exited. The overall strategic position of this business could be greatly improved.

Note that targeting the capability gap does not, at this stage, specify the *means* of how it will be achieved. That is left for the strategic options in the next section.

Improving distribution is an example of targeting a capability gap. Switching to a new distributor is a strategic option.

Lowering production costs across all segments is targeting a capability gap. Outsourcing or offshoring is a strategic option.

Strategic repositioning: an example

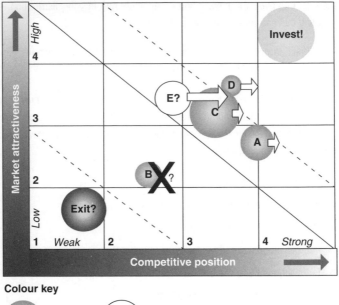

Colour key

Current segment   New segment   Impact of performance improvement options

Note: Diameter of bubble proportional to profit (except for segment E)

RE-BEERTH!

You inherit a long disused brewery sited in the heart of Barcelona, along with a nineteenth century brand name that has been long dormant, following liquidation and cessation of production in the late 1970s. It is a brand remembered fondly by older folk, but unknown to young people. What do you do? Where do you start in bridging this capability chasm?

You do what the Moritz family did. You relaunch the brand as youthful, social-media-friendly and ultra-Catalan (never mind the product now being brewed under licence in the neighbouring province of Aragon!). You transform the old brewery into a destination, the Fabrica Moritz Barcelona, a 'hotspot', a place to see and be seen. Framed by vaulted ceilings and space-age lighting, decorated by glistening beer vats and gilded barley ears, you install a beer museum, a micro-brewery, a 'concept store', a space for cultural events and a restaurant offering gourmet tapas at affordable prices – washed down, *es clar*, with freely flowing Moritz beer.

You grow revenues to around €50 million, though, unsurprisingly, given the €30 million investment in transforming the brewery, your P&L remains in the red. But you are in it for the long haul. You envisage further nibbling into the market share of the Big Three Spanish brewers, Heineken, Mahou-San Miguel and Damm – especially beyond the borders of Catalonia – and a healthy bottom line by 2020. Thence into the brand's third century . . .

Salut!

Targeting the gap for a startup

We concluded above that the secret to a successful startup is to hit the ground running with an evident competitive advantage.

But how defensible is that advantage?

If your new venture succeeds, you will be targeted. Competitors will eye your newly carved space with envy. They will come after you. And soon.

Remember the definition we used for strategy: strategy is how a company deploys its scarce resources to gain a sustainable advantage over the competition. The all-important word for a startup is *sustainable*.

How will you protect yourself against the inevitable competitive response? There are a number of ways you can try and sustain your competitive advantage:

- Patent protection of key products.

- Sustained innovation, staying one step ahead in product development.

- Sustained process improvement, staying one step ahead in cost competitiveness and efficiency.

- Investment in branding, identifying in the mind of the customer the particular benefit brought by your offering with its name.

- Investment, for business-to-business ventures, in customer relationships.

The process for determining your strategy to counteract competitive response, however, is the same as for an established business above.

In profiling the ideal player, you should include in your envisioning a scenario where there is a ferocious competitive response to your presence from the competitor, direct or indirect, that you most fear.

In specifying the target gap, you must go for goal – becoming the ideal player in your chosen niche market.

You must identify the capability gap between where you will be at launch and where the ideal player will be three to five years' hence.

That is the gap you will target. Nothing less will do. The vast majority of new businesses fail in the first five years. You either eat or be eaten. You have to go for it, go for goal.

In the next section we shall look at how your new venture will set out to bridge the capability gap and sustain its competitive advantage.

SIMPLE TIP

Strategic gap analysis has its critics. Capabilities, they say, are not as easily developed as resources. And rectifying weaknesses may be less value enhancing than building on strengths. These are perfectly valid points – but use gap analysis along with your common sense.

DA VINO A GELATO

In May 2007, a queue wound its way for 100 yards down Broadway in the heart of New York City. This eager throng was lining up not to marvel at the latest blockbuster movie but to indulge in an ice cream!

The idea had come five years earlier in Turin. A young winemaker, Guido Marinetti, was reading an article by Carlin Petrini, founder of the International Slow Food Movement, lamenting the fact that traditional gelato was no longer to be found in Italy. By that, he meant high-quality *gelato*, with fresh seasonal fruit mixed with organic milk and eggs, with no artificial aromas, thickening agents or colourings. 'Let's make it!' said Guido to his friend, Federico Grom. And they did.

In May 2003, they opened the first Grom gelateria in the centre of Turin. Despite high prices, queues formed daily outside the store, encouraging the entrepreneurs to open new stores in Padua, Florence and Parma. But now they found themselves with a capability gap.

They were selling their product on the basis of best possible quality, the same pitch as Guido had taken with selling his family's Barolo wine, but the rapid growth of the business was making it difficult to source guaranteed organic fresh fruit, with absolutely no use of pesticides, fertilisers or preservatives.

So they resolved to bridge the gap. They bought a Piedmont vineyard, chopped down the vines, planted their own fruit trees and bushes and learnt fast to supply themselves with the best, organic, seasonally specific fruit. These they fed into the organic liquid mixes in their Turin lab, to be frozen and distributed to the retail outlets, where they would be defrosted and whipped freshly every day.

This model helped Grom expand across Northern Italy and it even worked fine for the export market, with stores opening in New York, Paris and elsewhere.

▶

But further development prospects now meant the company needed to be managed as a big business. The two partners sold out to Unilever in 2015, but stayed on to ensure the maintenance of the brand's high standards and to guide international expansion.

I scream, you scream, the world screams for Grom?

Bridging the gap: business strategy

Don't be afraid to take a big step. You can't cross a chasm in two short jumps.

David Lloyd George

You have identified and targeted the strategic gap. Now you need to bridge it.

We will start with business strategy only and examine this in five sections:

1 Opting for a generic strategy.

2 Strategic repositioning and shaping profit growth options.

3 Grouping into strategic alternatives.

4 Making the strategic investment decision.

5 Bridging the gap for a startup.

We start with the generic strategies.

Opting for a generic strategy

Three generic business strategies have been with us since the early 1980s and should still form the starting point in your strategy development – see the figure below.

Three generic strategies for competitive advantage

They are strategies of:

- cost leadership;
- differentiation;
- focus.

Any one of these strategies can yield sustainable competitive advantage. Pursue two or all three of these strategies in the same business and you will end up 'stuck in the middle' – a recipe for long-term underperformance.

What is the primary source of competitive advantage in your business? Is it cost? Or is it the distinctiveness of your product and/or service offering?

Think back to the start of Part 2 where you rated your business against the factors for success in your industry. Did your business get higher ratings against the cost or the differentiation factors?

And go back one stage further. In Part 1 you identified and weighted these success factors in each key segment. Did you give a higher weighting to differentiation factors than to cost factors? Or the other way round?

There is little to be gained in being a cost leader in a segment that is not price-sensitive. Likewise, in being a highly differentiated producer in a segment where customers perceive little differentiation and demand only least cost.

If cost factors are most important in your business *and* you rated well or at least promisingly against them, then you should opt for a strategy of cost leadership.

If differentiating factors are more important *and* you rated well or at least promisingly against them, you should pursue a strategy of differentiation.

Either strategy can yield a sustainable competitive advantage. Either you supply a product (or service) that is at lower cost to competitors or you supply a product that is sufficiently differentiated from competitors that customers are prepared to pay a premium price for it – where the incremental price charged adequately covers the incremental costs of supplying the differentiated product.

For a ready example of a successful low-cost strategy, think of Southwest Airlines, where relentless maximisation of load factor enables it to offer seats at scarcely credible prices compared with those that prevailed before it entered the scene. And it still makes a profit. Or think of IKEA's stylish but highly price-competitive furniture.

A classic example of the differentiation strategy is Apple: never the cheapest, whether in PCs, laptops, mobile phones or tablets, but always stylistically distinctive and feature-intensive.

Then there is the focus strategy. While acknowledging that a firm typically can prosper in its industry by following either a low-cost or differentiation strategy, one alternative is to not address the whole industry but narrow the scope and focus on a slice of it, a single segment.

Under these circumstances, a firm can achieve market leadership through focused differentiation leading, over time, to scale and experience-driven low-unit costs compared to less focused players in that segment.

The classic example of a successful focus strategy is Honda motorcycles, whose focus on product reliability over decades yielded the global scale to enable its differentiated, quality products to become and remain cost-competitive.

While we are on motorcycles, look at Harley Davidson's turnaround strategy. On the verge of being wiped out by the likes of Honda, Kawasaki, *et al.* in the 1970s, when some nicknamed it the Hardly Ableson, it opted to focus on the heavyweight segment and produce solid, throaty, cruiser bikes. This strategy pulled market share in the category back from under 20 per cent to over 50 per cent – and in the process created an iconic 'Easy Rider'-style brand, which has lasted to this day.

Be aware, though, that any generic strategy is vulnerable to shifting customer needs and preferences. No strategy should be set in stone.

If you pursue a low-cost strategy, beware of a shift in customer needs putting a greater emphasis on quality, for which customers are prepared to pay a higher price. An example is the cinema industry. For years, many chains followed a policy of shoving the customers into their 'flea pits', keeping costs down to a minimum. Customers deserted in droves, opting for the comfort of their living rooms and the ease of the video recorder. Today, some cinemas offer reclining seats and waiter service – the diametrically opposite concept to the flea pit, and a service many customers are prepared to pay for.

Likewise, if you pursue a strategy of differentiation, beware of changing customer preferences. Customers may be prepared to shift to a new entrant offering a product or service of markedly inferior quality to yours, but good enough and at a significant price discount. The classic example is that of low-cost airlines, originating in the USA and spreading rapidly to the UK, Europe and Asia, and forcing the full-service national carriers to radically rethink their business model.

The canny business will spot the emergent trend and open a new business, preferably under a new brand, so as not to blur the image of the parent brand in the eyes of the customer. They will pursue one generic strategy in one business and a different one in another.

There is, however, no guarantee of success in the new business, given that it will operate in an entirely different culture – viz. the ill-fated attempts by upmarket car makers to move into the mass, with Daimler Benz-Chrysler unadvisedly following the precedent of BMW-Rover.

But it is especially inadvisable to mix strategies in one business, even if you are doing so in different segments. By definition, a strategic business unit operates in segments that are inter-related – whether by offering the same or similar products or services or addressing the same or similar customer groups. One strategy in one segment coupled with another strategy in another segment can not only confuse the customer but again land you 'stuck in the middle'.

SIMPLE TIP

Go for one generic strategy or the other. Low cost or differentiation. Do not do what so many companies do and try for both. They end up stuck in the middle of the road and getting run over.

NETS WORKING

There are many worthy business networking organisations. Many readers will, for example, have attended breakfast meetings with their local Business Network International (BNI) group.

But Australian Emma Isaacs happened upon an opportunity to pursue a classic differentiation strategy. Having run her own online recruitment business since she was 18, seven years later she was invited to attend a meeting of a small women's networking group, Business Chicks. It turned out to be for sale, so Emma bought it and set about transforming it into a nationwide support network and pressure group for women in business, offering meet-ups, events and online mutual support to its members – who have grown in numbers from

▶

just 250 upon acquisition to 44,000, along with 250,000 online supporters.

With annual membership fees of A$199, revenues may now exceed A$6 million. But Emma has reset her sights: in 2015, she relocated with her family to California to launch the business on its next phase of growth, Business Chicks USA.

Alas, there are few barriers to entry in online communities. Back home in Australia, entrepreneurs Gen George and Jane Lu spotted a niche within a niche and started 'Like Minded Bitches Drinking Wine'. Their network is 'open to girl bosses . . . and entrepreneurial girls . . . to share experiences, offer support . . . as well as celebrate wins and drown sorrows over copious amounts of wine.' They seem to have struck a chord: from launch in July 2015, and entering at the much lower price point of A$20, they have already signed up 27,000 members!

What next? A niche within a niche within a niche? Legless Ladies Loving Liebfraumilch?

Strategic repositioning and shaping profit growth options

You have set your generic strategy. What next?

You need to develop a series of profit growth options consistent with that strategy to bridge the strategic gap identified earlier in Part 2.

In targeting the portfolio gap, you applied the attractiveness/advantage matrix to your business and concluded that you should invest in certain segments, hold in others and perhaps exit one or two – and, conversely, perhaps enter one or two new ones.

You also targeted the capability gap that needs to be bridged for your firm to achieve your target level of competitiveness in selected segments.

Now you will determine how to bridge the capability gap with profit growth options in each key segment to be invested in. Likewise for segments to be held – and perhaps even for those slated for exit. And you will consider the business as a whole and how it can be reshaped in line with your strategy to generate sustained profit growth.

Finally, you will differentiate between actions you can take now to increase profit in the short term (next 12 months) and those that will improve strategic position and grow profits in the long term.

Having drawn up a range of profit growth options, you will evaluate them to decide which investment alternatives will yield the greatest return towards the goals and objectives of your firm.

Start by taking one segment at a time. Take those segments you have marked out for investing in, and then move on to those for holding, exit and entry. Finally, look at profit growth options that apply to all segments.

And always bear in mind the overall aim. Strategy is how a company deploys its scarce resources to gain a sustainable competitive advantage over the competition. Here you are deciding in which segments and on which initiatives you should allocate those resources – to deliver that sustainable competitive advantage.

In *which* segments and on *which* INITIATIVES should you allocate scarce resources to deliver **sustainable competitive advantage?**

Segments for investment

Take your largest segment, the one that gives the greatest contribution to overhead.

You have identified the capability gap in this segment. What are the options for bridging it?

- The gap may be in new product speed to market. Bridging it may require streamlined processes. You may need to invest in expert advisers.

- The gap may be in product reliability. Bridging it may require investment in new equipment, both in production and testing.

- The gap may be in customer service. Bridging it may require investment in staff and training, even a cultural shift, achievable only through a controlled change management programme.

In each of these examples, bridging the capability gap is a long-term process. That is often the case, but some profit growth options have faster results.

Indeed, you should be on the lookout for short-term profit growth options. There is nothing like a quick win or two following a strategy development process to gladden the boss's heart, justify the investment in time and energy and build team morale.

The quick win could come from a new angle in marketing, in its broadest sense – product, promotion, place, price – revealed in the strategy development process.

One such angle could be to lower prices. But that would reduce profit, not grow it, you might think. Perhaps, but maybe not for long:

- Volumes sold should increase, depending on the sensitivity (or technically 'price elasticity') of demand for the product, holding or growing revenue.

- Market share will be gained, enhancing your presence in the market and potentially stimulating further volume growth.

- Economies of scale may kick in, lowering your unit costs and restoring your operating margin (and even gross margin, if your greater volumes enable you to drive down the unit costs of bought-in materials, components and sub-assemblies).

These are some of the profit growth options, both short and long term, for bridging the capability gap in segments you will invest in. They are summarised in the figure below.

Strategic repositioning and performance improvement options

Strategic repositioning options by segment	Performance improvement options	
	Short term	**Long term**
Invest	• Marketing • Lower pricing to gain share?	Bridge capability gap, invest in: • Fixed and current assets • Business processes • Staff & training
Hold	• Reduce variable cost • Tweak pricing?	• Reduce variable cost • Re-compete? • Alliance?
New	• Prepare project plan	• Leverage strengths
Exit	• Improve financials?	• Withdraw (sell?)
Whole business	• Benchmark overhead • Marketing	• Reduce overhead • BPR, outsourcing, etc. • Resource-based investment

Next, you consider the profit growth options for those segments that you have chosen for holding – probably not to invest in, but definitely not to withdraw from.

Segments for holding

Holding on in a segment does not mean doing nothing, taking no strategic action. You need to actively manage your segment position and, preferably, strengthen it.

In the long term there are three profit growth options you should consider:

● **Reduce variable cost** – if you stand still on cost, you run the risk of a competitor undercutting you over time; an ongoing programme of cost reduction would be wise, whether in purchasing or operational efficiency.

- **Recompete** – change the rules of the game in some way, so that, effectively, you create a new segment out of the old; easier said than done, but it has been done again and again – think of a specialist retailer like Pets at Home, which has stolen share from traditional pet shops, supermarkets and DIY chains through offering not just a vast range of pet supplies but a destination in itself, with its rabbit, guinea pig and tropical fish displays captivating customers young and old; or in manufacturing, look for inspiration to the iPhone, so much more than a mobile phone.

- **Alliance** – you have a favourable competitive position in a segment that is moderately attractive; perhaps by allying with a competitor you could jointly have a stronger position in that segment and enable superior profit growth prospects for both parties.

In the short term, there are other options for you to consider. Cost reduction is both a short- and long-term option, but you may also consider tweaking your pricing in the segment, whether up or down:

- Nudging pricing up may change customer perceptions and give the impression that you are a premium player, though again you should think carefully on the price elasticity of demand; there are many examples of this strategy, such as the plethora of 'premium' lager brands in the UK, in reality bog standard, mass market beers in their home countries of Belgium, Germany, France, Italy, Jamaica, Mexico, Singapore, China – the list is endless, with so many playing the same game.

- Nudging pricing down, again depending on price elasticity, may gain you some extra volume and share, but beware of competitive retaliation.

Segments for exit

Profit growth options in those segments you have chosen to exit is limited. In corporate strategy, exiting a business unit can generate value through a structured sale process, including preparing the business for sale (the so-called 'dressing the bride') and improving the financials pre-sale. In business strategy, your presence in the business segments you choose to exit may have no sale value.

But there may be elements of value in that segment that can find a buyer. There may be some physical assets to sell or even some intangibles, such as use of the brand name in that segment.

Segments for entry

You may have identified new segments your firm should consider entering. These should be segments where you can leverage your existing strengths.

A new product/market segment should be synergistic with your existing business, having one or more of these characteristics:

- It is a new product (or service) related to your existing product range and sold to the same customer group.
- It is the same product but sold to a related customer group. (Remember that, if it is both a new product *and* is being sold to a new customer group, that greatly amplifies risk and would require a much tougher degree of substantiation.)
- It is a segment where success factors, both in cost and differentiation, mirror the relative strengths of your business.
- It is one in which some of your direct competitors are prospering and so might you.
- It is one in which some players in your line of business in other countries are prospering and there seems no reason why the same should not apply in your country.

In the short term, you need to prepare a robust project plan for new segment entry and improve the odds on securing long-term profit growth.

All segments

Finally, you need to consider profit growth options that apply across all segments in your business.

Long-term options may include:

- reducing overhead costs, having benchmarked them against your competitors;

- improving key business processes, perhaps through redesigning them;

- outsourcing, perhaps even offshoring, business processes such as IT, technical support and customer services;

- investing in the core competences of your business, whether they be in R&D, operations or sales;

- marketing – leveraging the name of your business across all segments, which is also a potential profit growth option in the short term.

Grouping into strategic alternatives

By now you should have a whole range of profit growth options. The danger is that it may look like a laundry list.

It should help to group them into two or three strategic alternatives. Each will represent a defined and coherent strategy for bridging the strategic gap in this business. One alternative may reflect investment primarily in one segment, another may reflect investment spread across a combination of segments and business-wide processes.

They should be mutually exclusive – you can follow one or another, but not both (or all). You can follow just the one alternative.

Grouping into strategic alternatives makes evaluation more manageable. Rather than evaluating 20 profit growth options, you will be evaluating two or three strategic alternatives.

SIMPLE TIP

Take care with the drawing up of profit growth options. The list should not get out of control.

Each option should satisfy two fundamental criteria:

- It should be consistent with your strategy.
- It should seem like a sound investment in itself.

Grouping the options into strategic alternatives further helps manage the process.

ENT-ERPRISE!

Are your child's pesky tonsils playing up? Has your doctor recommended they come out? How about taking your child to an organisation that specialises in doing just that? Oh, and by the way, will charge you about one third below the national average?

Meet ENT Institute (ENTI), a medical organisation operating out of 15 locations around Atlanta, Georgia that does what it says in the name – it specialises in the treatment of ear, nose and throat complaints. Period.

If your child is suffering from pimples, do not go there. If his or her knee gets twisted on the football field, go elsewhere. But if it is to do with the E, N or T, take a look at the website, where a full menu of treatments and charges is displayed transparently.

This is a classic, if smallscale, example of the focus strategy. ENTI's offering is not only highly differentiated – a centre of excellence in ENT for the state of Georgia, but its dedication to the specialism has enabled it to drive down costs to a level well below those of general hospitals – despite each of its five ENT specialist doctors earning over $1 million from a turnover of $27 million.

Keep your ears pricked as ENTI looks to neighbouring states . . .

Uncontested market space

One of the criticisms long aimed at industry analysis (see Part 1 and 'Gauging competitive intensity') is that it is too confined, too narrow in focus. The delineation of industry boundaries for analysis and the shaping of a competitive strategy within that industry may constrict the strategist so rigidly that the opportunity for genuine value innovation *beyond current industry boundaries* may be lost.

Two INSEAD academics, Chan Kim and Renée Mauborgne, argue that competing head-on in today's overcrowded industries results in nothing but a 'bloody red ocean of rivals fighting over a shrinking profit pool'. Based on a study of 150 strategic moves over a 100-year period, they argue that tomorrow's winners will succeed not by battling in red oceans but by creating 'blue oceans of uncontested market space ripe for growth'.

In a red ocean, you fight competitors with tooth and nail in an existing market space. In a blue ocean, you swim jauntily in an uncontested market space – new demand is created and competitors become irrelevant.

Such strategic moves create genuine 'value innovation', or 'powerful leaps in value for both firm and buyers, rendering rivals obsolete'.

They quote examples such as Apple's iTunes and Cirque du Soleil. Apple created a new market space by teaming up with the music companies to offer legal online music downloading, thereby consigning pioneer Napster (the bane of the music companies) to history. Cirque du Soleil reinvented the circus industry by blending it with ballet to create a new market space.

They further argue that the conventional choice of generic strategy between differentiation and low cost is also sub-optimal. That is the traditional choice faced by competitors in a red ocean. Blue ocean strategy enables the firm to do both, offering a differentiated product to a new market space at a cost sufficiently low to deter further entrants.

The holy grail of blue ocean strategy is to create: differentiated product + low cost = value innovation.

They put forward six principles for creating and capturing blue oceans:

- Reconstruct market boundaries.

- Focus on the big picture.

- Reach beyond existing demand.

- Get the strategic sequence right.

- Overcome organisational hurdles.

- Build execution into strategy.

Kim and Mauborgne challenge you to rethink fundamentally the rules of the game in your industry. The success factors you drew up in Part 1 may need to be radically rethought, perhaps even, and this is their first port of call, eliminated:

- Which factors that the industry takes for granted should be *eliminated*?

- Which factors should be *reduced well below* the industry's standard?

- Which factors should be *raised well above* the industry's standard?

- Which factors should be *created* that the industry has never offered?

In short, how can these success factors be revised so that a new value curve is created, one that breaks the trade-off between differentiation and low-cost strategies?

▶

The model is highly stimulating, but to be applied with care, especially for small- and medium-sized enterprises. Nine times out of ten, strategy development will be about improving strategic position in red ocean markets. Blue ocean markets may exist, but they are riskier – often greatly riskier. For every Apple iTunes and Cirque du Soleil, there are scores of attempted blue ocean strategies that have foundered.

Blue ocean thinking should be embraced, but subjected to the rigours of risk analysis found in Part 3 of this book.

Making the strategic investment decision

You have drawn up two or three strategic alternatives aimed at bridging the strategic gap in your business. They were mutually exclusive, so you can take only one of them. How do you evaluate them and select the best?

The answer is straightforward, in theory. You should choose the alternative that gives you *the highest return for the lowest risk*.

How you get there is not so straightforward. There is a spectrum of methods, ranging from the dangerously complex – real option valuation – to the dangerously simple – impact on earnings.

In the interests of keeping strategy plain and simple, you may opt for the payback method. It has its faults, many of them, but its virtue is its simplicity. As long as you use it with care, this method should, for the most part, do the job – see the figure below.

The payback approach to evaluating strategic alternatives

		Strategic alternatives		
	Unit	A	B	C
Financial benefits				
Investment costs = I	£000			
Average annual cash benefits over 5 years = B	£000/year			
Payback = I/B	Years			
Total cash benefits over 5 years = TB = B × 5	£000			
Net benefits = TB − I	£000			
Risk	L/M/H			
Non-financial benefits		•	•	• ....
		•	•	• ....
Non-financial disbenefits		•	•	• ....
		•	•	• ....

Work out the cost of the investment, say £I. Assess the annual benefits from the investment, namely the difference between the extra cash inflow (from revenues) and the extra cash outflow (from expenses) generated each year as a result of the investment. If the annual benefits are different each year, take their average over the first five years, £B/year. Divide B into I, and this gives you the 'payback', the number of years taken for the cash costs of the investment to be recouped.

If payback is *four years* or fewer, that could well be a sound investment. But do not jump on it. Work out the payback on the other strategic alternatives as well. They may have an even lower payback.

If you believe your investment is going to give you a longer-term advantage, and could last all of ten years, then an investment with a longer payback may still be beneficial. You might give serious consideration to an investment with a payback of six to seven years. It will be riskier, of course, because all sorts of things could happen to your competitive position over time.

Next work out the 'net benefits' of the strategic alternative, the total benefits over the five years less the investment cost.

The most promising alternative should be the one with the highest net benefits and with an acceptable payback.

Note that the alternative with the fastest payback is not necessarily the best – net benefits may be too small, even though they are the most rapidly achieved. But, if the alternative with the fastest payback is not mutually exclusive with the one that has the highest net benefits, perhaps you could do both?

Now for the caveats:

- Do not take account of the cash already invested in an alternative – this is history, so-called 'sunken costs'; only account for new cash that needs to be invested.

- Remember the time value of money – cash flows in Year 5 are not worth as much to you today as those in Year 1, so beware lumpy cash flows.

- The payback method is not kind to those alternatives with a longer gestation period, with cash generated mainly beyond the payback period.

- Do not forget your non-financial goals, which may be affected by one or more of the alternatives.

- Above all, do not forget risk – it is most unlikely that each alternative will carry the same degree of risk.

If your strategic investment decision is complex, and especially if benefits are late developing, do it properly through discounted cash flow analysis. If you do not feel comfortable with that, engage a specialist.

The strategic investment decision is seldom clear-cut. The financials are often hard to evaluate and even then there may be a trade-off between financial return, risk and meeting non-financial goals.

The decision is yours.

ONE HAPPY CHRISTMAS

The capability gap looked infinite one Christmas when Mac Harman's visiting brother-in-law kept sneezing – he was allergic to the Christmas tree. Mac offered to replace it with a top quality, identical artificial one, but could not find one – none such existed. All artificial trees looked, well, just that.

That gave Mac an idea. He travelled to China and soon had designs for highly realistic, if pricey, imitations of the likes of the Norway Spruce, the Nordmann Fir and the Silverado Slim. He imported 5,000 units in October 2006, set up a website and a pop-up stall in Stanford, California – and sold out well before Christmas!

Balsam Brands now sells high-quality trees, wreaths, garlands and ornaments and turns over $90 million, with operations extended to Europe and the Far East. Mac had spotted a product gap and filled it.

His favourite carol? *O Christmas tree, O Christmas tree, much pleasure thou canst give me*?

Bridging the gap for a startup

Earlier in Part 2, we targeted the gap between your competitive position upon launch and that of where you need to be three years out – by when your competitive advantage must have become, or is due to become, sustainable.

But how to get there?

There is nothing special here about a startup. In bridging the strategic gap, the process is the same as for an established business:

- **Confirm your generic strategy** – low cost or differentiated; do not opt for a focused strategy, you run the risk of being stuck in the middle – medium cost, medium differentiation, a recipe for business failure; a focused strategy is a luxury afforded to a more mature company with economies of scale; for a startup, be low cost or differentiated and do not waiver.

- **Shaping profit growth options** – crafting a set of initiatives to bridge the gap in the segments to be invested in, including those needed to protect yourself against competitive response; for a startup, of course, all segments are new and to be invested in – there are, by definition, as yet, no segments for holding or exit; group them into two or three strategic alternatives.

- **Evaluate the alternatives** – perhaps using the payback method described above.

To reiterate, to survive your launch, you must have a distinct competitive advantage – with a low-cost or differentiated strategy. To survive three to five years out, that competitive advantage must have become sustainable.

To summarise Part 2 on creating competitive advantage in a business:

- **Track your competitive position:** how are you placed?
- **Target the gap:** where should you be placed?
- **Bridge the gap:** how should you get there?

Creating competitive advantage in a business

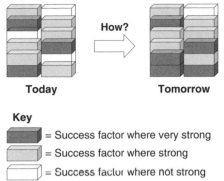

Today   **Tomorrow**

Key

= Success factor where very strong

= Success factor where strong

= Success factor where not strong

Another way of summarising business strategy can be seen in the figure above: how to strengthen your competitiveness against those success factors of greatest importance in the future.

But what if your company has more than one business? That is for the next chapter.

Bridging the gap: corporate strategy

The way to become rich is to put all your eggs in one basket and then watch that basket.

Andrew Carnegie

I mean, if you put all of your eggs in one basket, boy, and that thing blows up, you've got a real problem.

Jerry Bruckenheimer

Is yours a multibusiness company?

If not, and yours is a single business company, please move on to Part 3, which addresses a final wrinkle: in your strategy to bridge the gap in your business, are the risks acceptable?

If yours is a multibusiness company, this chapter applies to you. In the preceding chapter, you sought to bridge the gap in each of your businesses through improving competitiveness. That was business strategy. Now for corporate strategy.

Corporate strategy asks three questions:

● Which businesses should you be investing (your scarce resources) in?

● Which businesses should you be acquiring or divesting?

● Which resources common to all businesses should you focus on?

The second question will be looked at in the next section on adding value in mergers, acquisitions and alliances. The third on the so-called resource-based view of strategy will follow.

But we will start with which businesses you should invest in – in other words, how you should optimise your corporate portfolio.

Business vs corporate strategy

One thing we should clarify is how this book approaches the two distinct, but related, fields of strategy: business strategy and corporate strategy. A business is defined as an entity with a closely interrelated product (or service) offering and a cost structure largely independent of other businesses. Thus, in a large corporation, a business may well have not only its own CEO, CFO, COO, CSMO and CIO, but its own CTO, head of all R&D in that business.

A business is a substantive enough entity to warrant drawing up its own strategy, independent of the strategies its fellow businesses may be drawing up. This is business strategy.

Corporate strategy is, in the first instance, how you allocate resources between your businesses. Which will you invest in, which will you hold for cash generation, which will you sell, which may you be forced to close down? This is corporate strategy as portfolio planning.

But corporate strategy is more than that. It is about how you strive to attain synergies between your businesses, how you create value in the centre, how you initiate a winning culture or capability that permeates the entire organisation. This is corporate strategy as allocating corporate resources.

Most of this book has been about business strategy. In this chapter, we address corporate strategy.

Optimising the corporate portfolio

In the early 1980s, the new CEO of General Electric, Jack Welch, asked management guru Peter Drucker for advice. The latter responded with two questions that, arguably, changed the course of Welch's tenure: 'If you weren't already in a business, would you enter it today? And if the answer is no, what are you going to do about it?'

This led directly to Welch's corporate strategic dictat that every one of GE's businesses had to be either No. 1 or No. 2 in its sphere. If not, it would be fixed, sold or shut. The strategy was brutal, but effective.

In considering which businesses you should invest in, you have already met one of the two main tools to do just that, the attractiveness/advantage matrix.

You used the tool in Part 2 to determine the optimal balance of segments within a business. Now you can use it again to determine the optimal balance of businesses within a company.

Just substitute the word 'business' for 'segment' in the matrix, rank each business by its overall market attractiveness (a weighted average of each segment's market attractiveness) and its overall strategic position (again), place them in the corporate attractiveness/advantage matrix and you should get a clear picture on:

- which businesses you should invest in;
- which businesses you should hold and improve performance in;
- which businesses you should exit;
- which new businesses you should enter.

Now do the same with another terrific tool, similar but with a different nuance – the Boston Consulting Group growth/share matrix (see box below) – and compare the results.

These matrices will help you to optimise your corporate portfolio of businesses.

The growth/share matrix

The Boston Consulting Group's growth/share matrix, along with its catchy menagerie of cows and dogs, is one of those strategy tools that have stood the test of time. It first appeared in the late 1960s and is used as widely today as ever.

Its aims are the same as those of the attractiveness/advantage matrix, charting the relative position of the businesses analysed to determine which are most worthy of investment.

Where it differs is in its choice of parameters:

- Instead of a somewhat subjective assessment of *market attractiveness*, it opts for one measurable parameter, *market demand growth*.

- Instead of a somewhat subjective assessment of *competitive position*, it opts for one measurable parameter, *relative market share*.

The growth/share matrix offers, in essence, an objective, measurable proxy for the attractiveness/advantage matrix.

Here is how to use it. Draw up a 2 × 2 matrix, with these axes:

- Relative market share along the x-axis; not market share in itself, but your market share relative to that of your *leading* competitor; market share on its own is no indicator of relative strength; having a market share of 20 per cent may be a strength in a highly fragmented market where your nearest competitor has 10 per cent and most other main competitors are in single figures, but that 20 per cent takes on a different complexion if you are in a concentrated market where the leader has 40 per cent; in the first market, your relative market share would be 2.0x, but in the second 0.5x – implying very different prospects for sustaining competitive advantage.

- Market demand growth along the y-axis, taken as the forecast annual average growth rate in real terms over the next three to five years (as derived in Part 1).

Plot your businesses accordingly and reveal the following:

- **The 'stars':** those businesses that are in the top right quadrant, with high share in a fast growing market.

- **The 'cash cows':** those in the bottom right quadrant, with high share in a slow growing market.

- **The 'question marks':** those in the top left quadrant, with low share in a fast growing market.

- **The 'dogs':** those in the bottom left quadrant, with low share in a slow growing market.

The growth/share matrix: an example

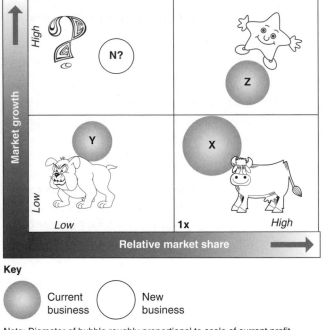

Key

○ Current business

○ New business

Note: Diameter of bubble roughly proportional to scale of current profit

Source: Adapted from the BCG Portfolio Matrix (**www.bcg.com**)

Note: The Boston Consulting Group's original matrix is displayed with the x-axis inverted and relative market share going from high to low. Here it has been taken from low to high, making it more readily comparable with the attractiveness/advantage matrix

Other things being equal, you should invest in the stars, harvest the cash cows, divest the dogs and analyse carefully the risks and returns of investing in the question marks.

Take an example – see the figure above. Here you may consider the following strategic options worthy of further analysis:

- Milking of cash cow X.
- Investment in star Z.
- Entry to question mark N.
- Harvesting or exit from dog Y.

How is the portfolio of businesses in your company? Hopefully your *main* businesses, from which you derive most revenues and/or profit, should find themselves positioned in the right-hand quadrants, the cash cows and stars. Any dogs? What should you do with them?

SIMPLE TIP

Whether your preference is to use the attractiveness/advantage matrix or the growth/share matrix, or both, in corporate portfolio analysis is up to you. But be aware of the limitations of each.

The former is criticised for being too subjective, the latter for being potentially misleading – market growth not necessarily being a proxy for market attractiveness (growth may be fast, but there may be a glut of competitors) and relative market share not necessarily being a proxy for competitive position (the market leader may be on the way down – think of fallen giants such as Nokia in mobile phones).

My advice is to use both matrices, observe any differences in the resultant conclusions and examine what lies beneath them.

FIRE SALE AT FORD

Top executives at Ford Motor Company's headquarters in Dearborn, Michigan faced an agonising decision in early 2007. Following a major downsizing operation in an attempt to readjust its cost base to operate profitably at lower volumes, it had recorded an unprecedented loss of almost US$13 billion the previous year. It had been forced to pledge most of its US assets, including its logo, as collateral to borrow $23 billion, yet it expected to burn through $17 billion of that in further losses through to 2009.

This was the price Ford was paying for years of failing to produce the small, fuel-efficient cars that US consumers increasingly preferred to purchase.

Now the executives needed to make an even more radical cash-generating decision – divestment. Its major divisions, such as Ford North America, Ford South America, Ford Europe and Ford Asia/Pacific-Africa, even Mazda of Japan, in which Ford had a 34 per cent stake, were all highly interlinked – in supply chain, product development, engineering and global marketing. Only one division was readily separable from the whole, Ford's Premier Automotive Group (PAG), which consisted of three business units – Aston Martin, Jaguar Land Rover and Volvo.

Yet PAG was also struggling, showing a $2.3 billion loss in 2006, though largely for different reasons. Ford had invested heavily in upgrading engineering and manufacturing capabilities, especially at Jaguar Land Rover, and expected the fruits of that investment to materialise over the next couple of years.

Nevertheless, the PAG businesses were put on the block. By the autumn of 2007, only six bidders had expressed interest in Jaguar Land Rover: four private equity firms and two Indian auto manufacturers. In March 2008, Tata Motors bought it for $2.3 billion, less than the $2.5 billion Ford paid for Jaguar alone in 1989 (let alone the $2.7 billion paid for Land Rover in 2000). Earlier, Ford had sold Aston Martin to Kuwaiti investors and, two years later, was to sell Volvo to Geely of China for $1.8 billion.

Ford claimed it had no choice but to sell its cash-draining PAG businesses when it did, though this was disputed by some analysts at the time, who argued that Ford should have done everything it could to hang on to PAG until it had returned to profit. Whatever the case, there is no doubt that this was an untimely divestment.

Jaguar Land Rover has since gone from strength to strength, largely on the back of Ford's efforts pre-sale, including in product development (viz. the successful Jaguar XF). In 2013 alone, the business made a profit of almost $4 billion. After seven successive years of growth, Jaguar Land Rover sold over 600,000 vehicles in the 12 months to March 2017, more than double volumes upon Tata's acquisition, and a sales target for the business of one million vehicles has been declared.

Divestment of one business unit to finance growth in another, or for an acquisition, is a fundamental tool of corporate strategy. But the success of the strategy often depends on the timing and the ability of the parent to 'dress the bride', to present the business for sale in the best possible light.

Creating value through mergers, acquisitions and alliances

Mergers, acquisitions and alliances (together M&A) have been with us since the dawn of capitalism. But, more often than not, they fail to create value.

The reason is simple: acquirers pay too much to gain control.

And the reasons behind that, long and well researched, are also clear:

- Managers are often hell bent on closing the deal – they have made up their minds this is what they want to do, for whatever reason, genuinely strategic or personal empire building, and they will not allow prolonged negotiations and an ever rising price tag to prevent them from getting the deal done.

- Managers do insufficient strategic analysis pre-deal.

- Managers do inadequate due diligence on the target.

- Managers underestimate the difficulties of post-deal integration and the inevitable delay in achieving aspired merger benefits.

The theory behind M&A value creation is simple. The extra value created through combining the two organisations (the 'synergy value') should be greater than the premium paid by the acquirer to gain control of the target.

Too often it is not.

Take care. Do not end up as one of the majority of acquirers who overpay.

SIMPLE TIP

Take great care in any merger, acquisition or alliance. Most fail!

Remember one of the eight principles preached by Tom Peters and Robert Waterman in *In Search of Excellence*, published in 1982: stick to the knitting.

Focus on what you know and do best.

This advice was reinforced by Chris Zook in his *Profit from the Core*. Successful companies operate in an FER cycle:

- Focus on, understand and reach full potential in the core business.

- Expand into logical adjacent businesses surrounding that core.

- Redefine pre-emptively the core business in response to market turbulence.

In other words, beware diversification, whether organically or through M&A.

SIMPLE TIP

Not only do most M&A deals fail to create value, but so too do most head offices! This was the path-breaking finding of Michael Goold, Andrew Campbell and Marcus Alexander in their 1994 book,

---

Corporate-Level Strategy: Creating Value in Multi-Business Companies. They found that the head office, or the corporate centre, more often than not failed to create value in a multibusiness company. It destroyed value.

One highly instructive insight emerges from their work, no matter the size of the firm. If another company can run one of your businesses better than you can, think of selling it to that company for a healthy sum and use the cash to build up another of your businesses, which you run better than others can.

'THERE IS A TIDE . . .'

'. . . in the affairs of men which, taken at the flood, leads on to fortune,' wrote William Shakespeare. Thirty miles up the road from his birthplace in Stratford-upon-Avon, Ford executives visiting Jaguar's plant at Castle Bromwich in 1989 might have heeded that advice.

Some, though by no means most, mergers or acquisitions have worked spectacularly well. Think of eBay's purchase of PayPal in 2002, which, when spun off 13 years later for $47 billion, returned eBay 30 times its money. Or Google's purchase of a mobile software house called Android for a mere $50 million in 2005. Or Facebook buying Instagram, a company that might otherwise have become its major competitor, in 2012 for $1 billion. Or Disney-Pixar, Adidas-Reebok . . .

We know, too, of acquisitions at the opposite end of the success spectrum, the financial catastrophes of AOL-Time Warner or Daimler-Chrysler or Microsoft-Nokia . . .

Tata Motors' purchase of Jaguar Land Rover, as we saw earlier in this section, must rank amongst the greatest hits, while Ford's earlier purchase of Jaguar and, later, Land Rover, ranks amongst the greatest misses.

▶

But that does not mean Ford was necessarily wrong to have bought these businesses, that Ford's corporate strategy had been misguided. Quite the contrary. Both moves were met at the time with largely positive reaction in the stock market.

At the end of the 1980s, the Detroit auto giants were anxious to upgrade their brands. GM linked up with Lotus, Chrysler with Maserati and Lamborghini, and Ford with Aston Martin, but these were niche high-performance operators, acquired to lend a touch of gloss to the volume brands.

Jaguar was a different proposition. It was an independent, quoted, medium-scale UK producer of luxury cars, competing with BMW and Mercedes in exports to the USA. It seemed too small to survive for long on its own and was in talks with potential partners, including Ford's arch rival, GM. Ford elbowed out others with a bid reflecting a 100 per cent premium on pre-bid stock price and described at the time by GM as 'unjustifiable'. In retrospect, GM did well to lose that battle.

Yet Ford saw a strategic fit and an opportunity to blend Ford expertise in volume car making in the sub-$20,000 market with Jaguar expertise in the over $40,000 market to produce a winner in the growing $30,000 market. Having sought earlier to do likewise with Alfa Romeo and later with Saab, Ford believed it had, at last, found the right partner.

One wonders, though, how much operational due diligence was undertaken. 'It wasn't that Jaguar's quality was bad, it was horrendous,' said Ford's first chairman of Jaguar, 'It was a terrible organisation making terrible cars.' He captured the attention of Jaguar workers by commenting that the only worse factory he had ever seen was the Gorky car plant in the old Soviet Union – where he had seen workers applying paint over bird droppings dumped on car roofs by pigeons happily flying around inside the plant!

Ford went on to invest heavily in Jaguar's plants and operations, even during the market downturn of 1991–3, as well as streamlining and upgrading the product line. By the mid-2000s, the quality of Jaguar cars was recognised in the industry as having been transformed from bottom to near the top.

Ford's acquisition of Jaguar was, therefore, not without strategic rationale. It was a long-term strategic investment, with Ford prepared to spend heavily on operational transformation and product development. But it became a catastrophic acquisition for two main reasons: Ford underestimated the difficulties, costs and duration of transforming archaic operations (estimates of Ford's total investment over 18 years run into the tens of billions of dollars) and Ford was unable to select the timing of its disposal of the business.

Had Ford's core business not been in such dire straits in 2008, and had Ford been able to hang on to its Jaguar Land Rover business until today, an orderly sale of the business in today's market might have achieved a reasonable return on Ford's strategically plausible, if ill-fated, investment.

Building strategically valuable resources

What 'strategically valuable resources' does your multibusiness company possess?

For a resource to be strategically valuable, David Collis and Cynthia Montgomery (*Competing on Resources*, 1995) conclude it needs to be:

- a distinctive competence – in other words, an activity that your firm not only does well, but better than others;
- hard to copy;
- long-lasting – for example, the evergreen Disney brand, which has outlasted the death of Walt by decades;
- hard to be appropriated – for example, by executives walking out of the door;
- unlikely to be substituted in the medium term.

You should invest in your strategically valuable resources, perhaps in three ways:

- **Invest in those you have** – for example, Disney reinvesting in animation.

- **Leverage those you have** – for example, Disney leveraging its brand name into retailing and publishing.

- **Upgrade those you should have** – for example, Intel moving into consumer branding with 'Intel Inside'.

You need, however, to take care with a resource-based corporate strategy. Building a unique set of resources and capabilities needs to be done in tandem with a sharp eye on the dynamic market context and competitive environment.

A corporate strategy that blends internally focused resource building and external awareness of the dynamic industry context can be powerful.

SIMPLE TIP

Take care. Successful companies are not necessarily those that possess the greater resources, but those that make best use of the resources they have. And working on weaknesses may not give as good a return as building on strengths.

3
Managing risk

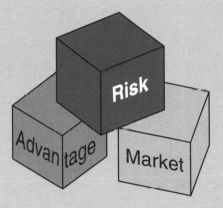

The biggest risk is not taking any risk . . . In a world that is changing really quickly, the only strategy that is guaranteed to fail is not taking risks.

Mark Zuckerberg

● Assessing the balance of risk and opportunity
● Containing risk

Risk is all around you. As in your personal life, so too with business. The trick is to understand it and contain it.

Each aspect of strategy development is subject to risk:

● Market demand takes a dip, wholly beyond your control.
● A competitor steamrollers into your market, regardless of the short-term cost.

- A key customer is acquired and you are ditched as a supplier.
- Your distribution partner goes under.
- Your new product launch flops.
- Your entry into a new market does likewise.

But before you give up the ghost, think on this: each risk may have a corresponding opportunity, viz.:

- Market demand receives a boost, again wholly beyond your control.
- A competitor withdraws from your market or goes under.
- A key customer acquires a major competitor and invites you to supply both.
- Your distribution partner expands and introduces new customers to you.
- Your new product launch succeeds beyond expectations.
- Your entry into a new market does likewise.

Phew! Life ain't so bad after all.

It is all about balance and judgement. And process. Read on. . .

Assessing the balance of risk and opportunity

When written in Chinese, the word 'crisis' is composed of two characters. One represents danger and the other represents opportunity.

John F. Kennedy

Here is what you do. Go through each part of the strategy development process again, especially the sections on market demand and industry competition, and pull out what seem to be the main risks and opportunities.

Assess them from two perspectives:

- How likely are they to take place – low, medium or high?
- If they do occur, how large an impact will they have – low, medium or large?

Now isolate what we shall term the 'big' risks and opportunities, as defined by those where the likelihood of occurrence is:

- medium (or high) and impact is high;
- high and impact is medium (or high).

You are now ready for these big risks and opportunities to be compared and assessed.

I first created the Suns & Clouds chart in the early 1990s. Since then, I have seen it reproduced in various forms in reports by my consulting competitors. They say imitation is the sincerest form of flattery, but I still kick myself that I did not copyright it back then!

The reason it keeps getting pinched is that it works. It manages to encapsulate in one chart conclusions on the relative importance of all the main strategic issues. It shows, diagrammatically and visually, whether the opportunities surpass the risks. Or vice-versa. In short, in one chart, it tells you whether your strategy is backable. Or not.

SIMPLE TIP

Whether or not you are seeking external funding, draw up your strategy and assess the balance of risk as if you were. Private equity investors are rigorous in their due diligence process and their approach to risk and return. They get things right far more often than not – otherwise they would be out of a job.

Ask yourself whether your strategy would be backable to external financiers, even if it is only to be presented internally to your board for go-ahead.

The Suns & Clouds chart (see on the next page) forces you to view each risk (and opportunity) from two perspectives: how likely it is to happen and how big an impact it would have if it did. You do not need to quantify the impact, but instead have some idea of the notional, *relative* impact of each issue on the value of the firm.

In the chart, risks are represented as clouds, opportunities as suns. For each risk (or opportunity), you need to place it in the appropriate position on the chart, taking into account both its likelihood and impact.

The chart tells you two main things about how backable your strategy is: whether there are any *extraordinary* risks (or opportunities) and whether the overall *balance* of risk and opportunity is favourable.

Extraordinary risk

Take a look at the top right-hand corner of the chart. There is a heavy thundercloud in there, with two exclamation marks. That is a risk that is both very likely *and* very big. It is a showstopper risk. If you find one of them, your strategy is unbackable.

The Suns & Clouds chart

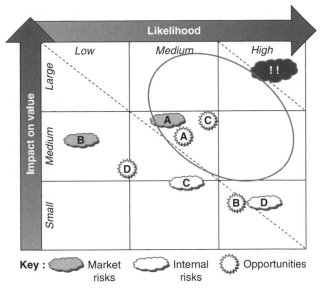

Key : Market risks   Internal risks   Opportunities

The closer a cloud gets to that thundercloud, the worse news it is. Risks that hover around the diagonal (from the top left to the bottom right corners) can be handled, as long as they are balanced by opportunities. But as soon as a cloud starts creeping towards that thundercloud, perhaps to around where opportunity C is placed, that is when you should start to worry.

But imagine a bright shining sun in the spot where that thundercloud is. That is terrific news, and you will have suitors clambering over each other to back you.

The balance of risk

In general, there is no showstopper risk. The main purpose of the Suns & Clouds chart will then be to present the *balance* of risk and opportunity. Do the opportunities surpass the risks? Given the overall picture, are the suns more favourably placed than the clouds? Or do the clouds overshadow the suns?

The way to assess a Suns & Clouds chart is to look first at the general area above the diagonal and in the direction of the thundercloud. This is the area covered in the Suns & Clouds chart by the parabola. Any risk (or opportunity) there is worthy of note. It is at least reasonably likely to occur *and* would have at least a reasonable impact.

Those risks and opportunities below the diagonal are less important. They are either of low to medium likelihood *and* of low to medium impact. Or they are not big enough, or not likely enough, to be of major concern.

Take a look at the pattern of suns and clouds in your chart around the area of the parabola. The closer each sun and cloud to the thundercloud, the more important it is. If the pattern of suns seems better placed than the pattern of clouds, your strategy may be backable.

In the chart above, there are two clouds and two suns above the diagonal. But risk D lies outside the parabola. The best placed is opportunity B. Risk A and opportunity A more or less balance each other out, likewise other risks and opportunities. Opportunity B seems distinctly clear of the pack. The opportunities seem to surpass the risks. The strategy looks backable.

One of the best features of the Suns & Clouds chart is that it can be made dynamic. If the balance of risk and opportunity shown on the chart is unfavourable, you may be able to do something about it– and the chart will show this clearly.

For every risk, there are mitigating factors. Many, including those relating to market demand and competition (the darker clouds in the Suns & Clouds chart), will be beyond your control. Those relating to your firm's competitive position, however, are within your power to influence. They may, indeed, be an integral part of your emergent strategy.

Likewise, your strategy may improve the likelihood of achieving a key opportunity on the chart, thereby shifting the sun to the right.

Risk mitigation or opportunity enhancement in the Suns & Clouds chart can be illuminated with arrows and target signs. They will show where your firm should aim for and remind you that it is a target. Your strategy should improve the overall balance of risk and opportunity in your firm.

You can use the Suns & Clouds chart in so many situations. It was designed for use in transactions such as acquisitions, alliances and investments, but it is just as useful in project appraisal, strategy review (as here) or even in career development and change. It might even have been useful in deciding whether or not to have backed Britney (see its application in 'Britney does it again' below).

What about highly improbable but potentially catastrophic risks, you might ask? And those that seem explicable, even justifiable, only in retrospect, termed 'Black Swans' by Nassim Nicholas Taleb (former trader and risk analyst) – like the 2008 financial meltdown? The chart deals with them, too.

In the autumn of 2001, my colleagues and I were advising a client on whether to invest in a company involved in airport operations. After the first week of work, we produced an interim report and a first-cut Suns & Clouds chart. In the top left-hand corner box, we placed a risk titled 'major air incident'. We were thinking of a serious air crash that might lead to the prolonged grounding of a common class of aircraft. It seemed unlikely, but would have a very large impact if it happened.

9/11 came just a few days later. We never envisaged anything so devastating, so inconceivably evil, but at least we had alerted our client to the extreme risks involved in the air industry. The deal was renegotiated and completed successfully.

SIMPLE TIP

Do not worry if your Suns & Clouds chart does not make that much sense initially. This chart changes with further thought and discussion. *Always.* Arguably, its greatest virtue is its stimulus to discussion. It provokes amendment.

Remember, you cannot be exact in this chart. Nor do you need to be. It is a pictorial representation of risk and opportunity, designed to give you a *feel* for the balance of risk and opportunity in your strategy.

BRITNEY DOES IT AGAIN

Who do you think was the highest paid woman in the music industry in 2012? According to *Forbes* magazine, it was not 1950s throwback Katy Perry, in at number five, nor the whacky Lady Gaga or the raunchy Rihanna, not even the runner-up, country crossover singer-songwriter, Taylor Swift.

The phenomenon that is Beyoncé, with her astonishing vocal range, stunning looks and Tina Turneresque command of the stage, soon to knock 'em dead at the SuperBowl XLVII Halftime Show, was not even in the top five.

No, it was the schoolgirl sensation from the late 1990s, back at the top with $68 million.

Britney stormed onto the music scene in December 1998 with *Baby One More Time*. The voice was good enough, as was the song, but it was the positioning of this 17-year-old that sealed the deal – with the video designed overtly to fuel the fantasies of every schoolboy and the aspirations of every schoolgirl – including my two. She became their goddess and, as soon as Britney brought out her first fragrance, Santa duly obliged.

History may tell us that this video marked a seminal moment in the sad but inexorable process of the sexualisation of schoolchildren, but it did the trick for Britney. She became the bestselling teenage artist ever and, by 2002, *Forbes* magazine was rating her as the world's most powerful celebrity.

But, in early 2004, came the first signs that something was amiss. She married a childhood sweetheart in Las Vegas and then annulled it within three days. She attended the Kabbalah sect of her role model, Madonna. She became engaged to a dancer and opened up their lives in a three-month reality show. They had two children, but sadly divorced within two years.

She became in her own words an 'emotional wreck'. She partied heavily with the likes of Paris Hilton, flirting with paparazzi and flagrantly displaying her absence of underwear. She shaved off all her hair. She checked in and out of drug rehabilitation centres. She lost custody of her children to her ex-husband. By early 2008, she was hospitalised and put under the conservatorship of her father.

If you were a music industry mogul in mid-2008, would you have backed Britney? The risks were huge. She had been a teen star like none other, but that was yesterday. At 27, she was passé, troubled and unreliable. Her looks had lost their freshness, her body had become maternal, her voice remained unexceptional. How could she compete with a Beyoncé?

Would you have backed Britney in 2008?

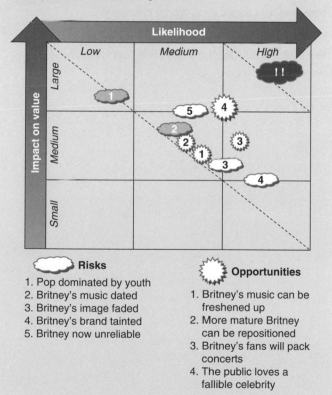

Risks
1. Pop dominated by youth
2. Britney's music dated
3. Britney's image faded
4. Britney's brand tainted
5. Britney now unreliable

Opportunities
1. Britney's music can be freshened up
2. More mature Britney can be repositioned
3. Britney's fans will pack concerts
4. The public loves a fallible celebrity

Let's look at her Suns & Clouds.

It would not have looked too good. Risks and opportunities seem more or less balanced out – with Britney's dated music, fading image, tarnished brand and unreliable character balanced by opportunities to freshen up the music, reposition her as more mature and to rely on the legion of diehard fans to show up when her concert comes to town, again like my daughters!

But one opportunity steals the show. The public loves a fallible celebrity. And any news is good news. As long as she could pull herself together, and perform when required, countering that risk, cloud no. 5, that opportunity, sun no. 4, should shine through to success.

And, yes, four years later, with her album *Femme Fatale* and the ensuing tour, oops, she did it again and hit us, baby, one more time.

Containing risk

Take calculated risks. That is quite different from being rash.

George S. Patton

There is one further use for your Suns & Clouds chart. It can highlight the scope for containing areas of risk in your strategy.

Strip out all the suns from your chart, leaving just the clouds, and superimpose four boxes, carefully located, containing the words 'accept', 'reduce', 'transfer' and 'avoid' – see the figure below.

Containing risk

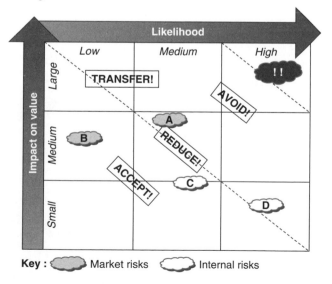

Key : ☁ Market risks ☁ Internal risks

Your four basic strategies for managing risk, then, are:

- Where at all possible, *avoid* the big risks – if it is an internal risk, do not do it; if it is a market risk, withdraw.

- Where it is not possible to avoid a big risk, *transfer* it to your insurers.

- *Reduce* the medium risks through limitation, for example, through greater storage for supplies or more sophisticated systems or more data back-up.

- *Accept* the small risks.

Make sure, though, that the exercise does not grind you down. The trouble with many risk management tools is that they can be unbalanced. The beauty of the Suns & Clouds chart is that it acknowledges risk, but balances it with opportunity. A purely risk management chart like that above has no such balance and may seem like unremitting gloom.

Risks do need to be managed, but risk concern must not get in the way of developing a robust, challenging, value-enhancing strategy for your business.

Conclusion

You now have a strategy, a plain and simple strategy (see summary below), to guide your firm to the next level.

Your firm is now far better equipped for the future than it was before.

Michael Porter once wrote that, 'The company without a strategy is willing to try anything.'

Not yours. It will have direction. You will be facing the future with a strategy that will maximise your chances of achieving your goals.

You have the strategy you need for your business to succeed.

Strategy Pure and Simple: summary

Stage	Key tasks
Get ready!	• Pinpointing key segments
	• Setting long-term goals . . .
	. . . and SMART objectives
1 Understanding your market	• Sizing and forecasting market demand
	• Assessing industry competition
2 Creating competitive advantage	• Tracking competitive position
	• Targeting the strategic gap
	- Portfolio and capability gaps
	• Bridging the gap
	- Opting for a generic strategy
	- Repositioning
	- Grouping into alternatives
	- Making the investment decision
3 Managing risk	• Assessing the balance of risk and opportunity
	• Containing the risk
Get going!	• Implementing the strategy

The Strategy Pyramid

In this book I have applied the KISS principle (Keep it simple, stupid) to strategy development. In earlier books, *Key Strategy Tools* (2012) and *The Financial Times Essential Guide to Developing a Business Strategy* (2013), I set out a more comprehensive strategy development process called the Strategy Pyramid.

This consisted of nine building blocks (see the figure below):

1 Knowing your business.

2 Setting goals and objectives.

3 Forecasting market demand.

4 Gauging industry competition.

5 Tracking competitive advantage.

6 Targeting the strategic gap.

7 Bridging the gap with business strategy.

8 Bridging the gap with corporate strategy.

9 Addressing risk and opportunity.

The strategy pyramid is a rational, coherent and proven approach to strategy development. But it has one defect: it has nine building blocks. Some people find it hard to remember nine of anything. Psychologists tell us that three is the number of items that the human brain can best process and recall.

So, the first step in applying the KISS principle to strategy development had to be to reduce the nine blocks to three stages – see the following figure.

The Strategy Pyramid

Source: Evans, V. (2012) *Key Strategy Tools.* FT Publishing.

From Strategy Pyramid to KISSTRATEGY

The Strategy Pyramid	KISSTRATEGY
Block 1: Knowing your business Block 2: Setting goals and objectives	[Getting ready]
Block 3: Forecasting market demand Block 4: Gauging industry competition	**1 Understanding the market**
Block 5: Tracking competitive position Block 6: Targeting the strategic gap Block 7: Bridging the gap with business strategy Block 8: Bridging the gap with corporate strategy	**2 Creating competitive advantage**
Block 9: Addressing risk and opportunity	**3 Managing risk**

Blocks 1 and 2 are really preparatory steps, getting ready for the strategy process. So, they can be treated as an introduction to strategy formulation.

Blocks 3 and 4 represent the assessing of demand and supply in the market, the 'micro-economy' in which your firm operates.

Blocks 5 through to 8 all represent the building of your firm's enduring competitive advantage.

And Block 9 is about checking that the risks in your strategy are manageable.

So, there we have it: the three essential parts of strategy development:

1   Understanding the market.

2   Creating competitive advantage.

3   Managing risk.

It is no coincidence that these three parts satisfy the perspectives of three distinct sets of stakeholders, each of whose hats I have worn at different stages of my career.

As an economist, strategy needs to be harmonious with the market in which the firm operates, the so-called 'micro-economy'. As a business strategist, strategy must focus on creating an enduring competitive advantage. As a financier, strategy has to address, manage and contain risk.

Put all three parts together and you have a straightforward, yet comprehensive approach to strategy development.

This is KISSTRATEGY. This is strategy plain and simple.

Cracking the jargon

Business A strategic business unit, a profit centre entity with a closely inter-related product (or service) offering and a cost structure largely independent of other businesses.

Business strategy Gaining a sustainable competitive advantage for a single business.

Capabilities How a firm deploys its resources.

Capability gap The gap in performance between where your firm is currently positioned against success factors and where it aims to be.

Competitive advantage The strategic advantage possessed by one firm over others in a product/market segment or industry that enables it to make superior returns.

Competitive intensity The degree of competition in a given industry and a main determinant of industry profitability.

Competitive position A rating of a firm's relative competitiveness in a given product/market segment or industry.

Corporate strategy Optimising value from a portfolio of businesses and adding value to each through exploiting the firm's core resources and capabilities.

Customer buying criteria What customers need from their suppliers.

Economies of scale The reduction in unit costs in a firm arising from an increase in the scale of its operations.

Generic strategies Those that relate to an entire class of businesses, namely differentiation, low cost or focus strategies.

Industry maturity The stage of evolution of an industry, from embryonic through to growing, mature and aging.

Industry supply The aggregate supply by producers of a product (or product group) over a specified period of time, typically one year.

Issue A matter under discussion or in dispute, often due to future uncertainty – a risk or an opportunity.

Success factors What firms need to do to meet customer buying criteria and run a sound business.

Market attractiveness A composite measure of the relative attractiveness of a product/market segment, taking into account factors such as market size, market growth, competitive intensity, industry profitability and market risk.

Market demand The aggregate demands of customers for a product (or product group) over a specified period of time, typically one year.

Portfolio The collection of key product/market segments in a business or of businesses in a multibusiness company.

Resources A firm's productive assets, whether human, physical, financial or intangible, as distinct from capabilities, which are how a firm deploys its resources.

Segment A slice of business where the firm sells one product (or product group) to one customer group (strictly a 'product/market segment').

Stakeholder Persons and organisations with a non-shareholding stake in the success of the firm, for example, employees, customers, suppliers, national and local government, the local community.

Strategic repositioning Adjusting strategic position through investing, holding, exiting or entering segments (for business strategy) or businesses (for corporate strategy).

Strategy How a firm achieves its goals by deploying its scarce resources to gain a sustainable competitive advantage.

Structured interviewing Systemised (or systematic) interviewing of customers, suppliers and other industry observers to gain strategic information.

Synergy Where the whole is greater than the sum of the parts and, specifically in mergers, acquisitions and alliances, where the value of the merged entity is greater than the pre-bid standalone value of the acquirer plus that of the target/partner.

Ten books to read next

Clayton M. Christensen (1997) *The Innovator's Dilemma: When New Technologies Cause Great Firms to Fail*, Harvard Business School Press. How a firm can do everything right, yet still be destroyed by a disruptor.

Collins, J. (2001) *Good to Great: Why Some Companies Make the Leap . . . and Others Don't*, Random House Business. How vision and big, hairy, audacious goals drive business success.

Evans, V. (2013) *The FT Essential Guide to Developing a Business Strategy: How to Use Strategic Planning to Start Up or Grow Your Business*, FT Publishing. The original version of this book, with greater detail and a full case study throughout the book.

Evans, V. (2016) *KISSTRATEGY: A Keep-It-Simple Guide on How to Build a Winning Strategy for Your Startup or Small Business*, Business & Careers Press. The pocket-sized version of this book.

Goddard, J. and Eccles, T. (2012) *Uncommon Sense, Common Nonsense: Why Some Organisations Consistently Outperform Others*, Profile Books. Provocative: what did BMW spot in the Mini that previous owners had not?

Grant, R.M. (2015) *Contemporary Strategy Analysis*, Blackwell, 9th edn. The everlasting, definitive, yet readable textbook on strategy development.

Kim, W.C. and Mauborgne, R. (2005) *Blue Ocean Strategy: How to Create Uncontested Market Space and Make the Competition Irrelevant*, Harvard Business School Press. This century's challenge to Michael Porter: how to escape the bloody red ocean of industry rivalry.

Mintzberg, H. (1994) *The Rise and Fall of Strategic Planning*, Free Press. Iconoclastic, the 'suck-it-and-see' alternative to strategic planning.

Mullins, J. (2010) *The New Business Road Test: What Entrepreneurs and Executives Should Do Before Writing a Business Plan*, FT Prentice Hall, 3rd edn. The must-read book for those starting their own business.

Porter, M.E. (1980) *Competitive Strategy: Techniques for Analyzing Industries and Competitors*, Free Press. The rock of industry economics, upon which business strategy was founded.

Index

addressable market 4
addressed market 4
Adidas 93
Alexander, Marcus 92
alliance 72
Amazon 15
Android software 93
AOL 93
Apple 65, 76
Ashley Madison website 29–30
Aston Martin 90
attractive market segment 50–1
attractiveness/advantage matrix 50,
    68, 87
available market 4
awareness, changing 11

Baby One More Time (song) 104
balance of risk 101–3
bargaining power, supplier/customer 20
Black Swans 103
Blockbuster stores 21–2
blue ocean strategy 76–7
Boston Consulting Group
    growth/share matrix 86–9
bottom-up competitor sizing 4
bottom-up customer sizing 4
bottom-up market research 4
branding, investment in 60
Britney, Spears 104–6
Brooklyn Zoo, New York 45
Bruckenheimer, Jerry 84

business 113
Business Chicks 67–8
business strategy 113
    bridging the gap 63–83
    vs. corporate strategy 85
    grouping into strategic alternatives
        74–5
    opting for generic strategy 64–7
    for startup 81–3
    strategic investment decision 78–81
    strategic repositioning and shaping
        profit growth options 68–74
business structural shifts 11

Campbell, Andrew 92
capabilities 113
capability gap 113
    envisioning future scenarios 54
    profiling ideal player 54–5
    specifying 56–8
    stretching your sights 55–6
    targeting 49, 54–8, 69
Carnegie, Andrew 84
Chrysler 93, 94
cinema attendance 13–14
Cirque du Soleil 76
climate change 11
Collis, David 95
competition, acknowledging 30–3
    competitive response 32–3
    direct competition 31
    indirect competition 31–2

competitive advantage 46–7, 59–60, 64, 113
  business strategy 63–83
  corporate strategy 84–96
  creating 35–96
  sustainable 69
  targeting strategic gap 49–62
  tracking competitive position 37–48
competitive intensity 50, 113
  customer bargaining power 20
  environmental factors 20
  existence of substitute products or solutions 20
  internal rivalry 19–20
  supplier bargaining power 20
  threat of new entrants 20
competitive position analysis 113
  in established business 37–41
  example 39
  getting past first base 41–2
  implications for future market share 42
  implications for strategy development 42–3
  for startup 45–7
competitive response 32–3, 60
competitiveness
  by segment 40
  over time 40–1
competitors 19
containing risk 107–8
Corporate-Level Strategy: Creating Value in Multi-Business Companies (book) 93
corporate strategy 113
  bridging the gap 84–96
  building ?strategically valuable resources' 95–6
  vs. business strategy 85
  creating value through M&A 91–3

optimising corporate portfolio 85–6
  resource-based 96
cost competitiveness 26
cost leadership 64, 65
cost per click (CPC) 24
cost reduction 72
customer bargaining power 20
customer buying criteria, identifying 22–4, 25–6, 113
customer needs 23
customer survey meeting 24
cyclicality 50

Daimler 93
David Lloyd 44
demand drivers 13–14
demand risks 14
Detroit auto giants 94
differentiation-related success factors 26
differentiation strategy 64–5, 66
direct competition 31
Disney 93, 95–6
distribution, improving 57
Drucker, Peter 85

E2-R2-P2, of customer buying criteria 23–4
easyGym 44
eBay 93
economic cycle 11
economies of scale 70–1, 113
effectiveness, of product 23
efficiency, of service 23
ENT Institute (ENTI) 75
entrants, threat of new 20
entry, segments for 73
environmental factors 20
exit, segments for 72–3
extraordinary risk 100–1

Fabrica Moritz Barcelona 58–9
face competition 46
Facebook 93
fashion 11
fem-bots, in Ashley Madison website 30
Femme Fatale (album) 106
Fierce Grace 45
final triangulation 5
focus strategy 64, 65–6
Forbes magazine 104
Ford Motor Company 90–1, 94–5
future competitive position, example 41
future market share 42

Game of Thrones 15
Geely 90
General Electric 85
generic strategies 113
    confirming 82
    opting for 64–7
George, David Lloyd 63
George, Gen 68
Google 93
Goold, Michael 92
government policy 10
Grom, Federico 61
Grom gelateria 61–2
Gym Group 44
Gymbox 43–5

Harley Davidson 66
Harman, Mac 81
holding on in a segment 71–2
Honda motorcycles 66
HOOF (HDDF) approach 8–9, 11
Hot Yoga 45
Hulu 22

ideal player, profiling 54–5, 60
IKEA 65
indirect competition 31–2, 46

industry competition
    acknowledging competition in startup
        30–3
    assessing 18–33
    checking out competitors 19
    customer buying criteria, identifying
        22–4
    forces of 20
    gauging competitive intensity 19–22
    success, factors for 25–30
industry maturity 113
industry profitability 50
industry supply 113
innovation 60
Instagram 93
Intel 96
internal rivalry 19–20
investment 95
    segments for 70–1
Isaacs, Emma 67
issue 114

Jaguar 90, 91, 93–5

Kennedy, John F. 99
Kim, Chan 76–7
KISS (keep it simple, stupid) principle
        110–12
Kuwaiti investors 90

LA Fitness 44
Lamborghini 94
leveraging 96
Like Minded Bitches Drinking Wine 68
Lotus 94
low-cost strategy 66
Lu, Jane 68

management and market share,
        assessing 26–7
manufacturing efficiency 25

Marinetti, Guido 61
market
  attractiveness 50–1, 87, 114
  understanding 1–33
market demand 114
  assessing 8–15
  assessing demand for startup 15–17
  drivers future 9, 11
  drivers past 9, 10
  forecast growth 9, 11–12
  growth 16, 50, 87
  historic growth 9–10
  sizing market 3–8
market growth 6
market research 16, 17
market risk 50
market share 6, 26–7, 70
market share change 6
market size 3–8, 16, 50
market space, uncontested 76–8
marketcrafting 4, 8
  example 7
  seven steps in 5–6
Maserati 94
Mauborgne, Renée 76–7
mergers, acquisitions and alliances
  (M&A) 91–3
micro-economy 112
Microsoft 93
Milton Keynes 13–14
Montgomery, Cynthia 95
Mullins, John 47
multiplexes 13–14
Murdoch, Rupert 37
must-have success factor 28–30, 41

Napster 76
Nassim Nicholas Taleb 103
negative driver 14–15
net benefits 80
Netflix 15, 22

New Business Road Test, The (book) 47
No. 1 Ladies Detective Agency
  (novel series) 47–8
Nokia 93
nominal market demand growth 10

opportunities, and risks 99–103

patent protection 60
Patton, George S. 107
payback method, to evaluating strategic
  alternatives 78, 79, 82
PayPal 93
per capita income growth 10
Petrini, Carlin 61
Pixar 93
population growth 10, 11
Porter, Michael 109
portfolio 114
portfolio gap, targeting 49–53, 68
Premier Automotive Group (PAG) 90
premises 23
price 23, 26
price change 11
price elasticity 70, 72
process improvement 60
product functionality 25
product reliability 25
Profit from the Core (book) 92
profit growth options, shaping
  68–74, 82
Pure Gym 44

quantitative approach 27

range, of products and services 23
real market demand growth 10
recompete 72
red ocean strategy 76
reduce variable cost 71–2
Reebok 93

related market triangulation 4
relationship, with producer 23
resources 114
resources-based corporate strategy 96
risks
    managing 97–109
    and opportunities 99–103

scheduled delivery 25
screening success factor 30
segments 46, 114
    competing by 40
    for entry 73
    for exit 72–3
    for holding 71–2
    for investment 70–1
Shakespeare, William 49, 93
small and medium sized enterprises
    (SMEs) 3–4
Smith, Alexander McCall 48
Southwest Airlines 65
Sports Direct Fitness 44
stakeholder 114
startup
    assessing demand for 15–17
    bridging the gap for 81–3
    competitive position for 45–7
    targeting gap for 59–60
strategic alternatives, grouping into
    74–5
strategic gap analysis
    drawbacks 60
    targeting capability gap 54–8
    targeting gap for startup 59–60
    targeting portfolio gap 49–53
strategic investment decision, making
    78–81

strategic position 52–3
strategic repositioning 58, 114
    and shaping profit growth options
        68–74
strategically valuable resources 95–6
strategy 59, 114
    development 6, 13, 18, 42–3, 64,
        70, 97
    pyramid 110–12
structured interviewing 114
substitute products or solutions 20
success factors 54–5, 114
    in business 37–8
    in engineering niche market 41
    in industry 25–30
Sun Tzu 19
Suns & Clouds chart 99–106
supplier bargaining power 20
sustainability 59
switching costs 27
synergy value 92, 114

Tata Motors 90, 93
Time Warner 93
Tomlin, Lily 18
top-down market research 4
turnaround strategy 66

Virgin Active 44
volatility 50
Volvo 90

Welch, Jack 35, 85

Zook, Chris 92
Zuckerberg, Mark 97